T0396851

Formal Aspects *of* Chinese Grammar

Formal Aspects *of* Chinese Grammar

Jie Xu

University of Macau, China

World Scientific

NEW JERSEY · LONDON · SINGAPORE · BEIJING · SHANGHAI · HONG KONG · TAIPEI · CHENNAI · TOKYO

Published by

World Scientific Publishing Co. Pte. Ltd.
5 Toh Tuck Link, Singapore 596224
USA office: 27 Warren Street, Suite 401-402, Hackensack, NJ 07601
UK office: 57 Shelton Street, Covent Garden, London WC2H 9HE

Library of Congress Cataloging-in-Publication Data
Names: Xu, Jie, author.
Title: Formal aspects of Chinese grammar / Jie Xu.
Description: New Jersey : World Scientific, [2017] |
    Includes bibliographical references and index.
Identifiers: LCCN 2016053345| ISBN 9789813202900 | ISBN 9789813202917 (pbk)
Subjects: LCSH: Chinese language--Grammar, Comparative. |
    Chinese language--Reflexives. | Chinese language--Grammar.
Classification: LCC PL1099 .X8 2017 | DDC 495.15--dc23
LC record available at https://lccn.loc.gov/2016053345

British Library Cataloguing-in-Publication Data
A catalogue record for this book is available from the British Library.

Printed in Singapore

Preface

This book is a collection of articles published over the past decade by the author. These articles are concerned with various issues related to the formal aspects of Chinese grammar including possessor raising, null subject, null object, pied-piping in logical form, focus marker, question formation, and adverbial reflexive. Each article has made contribution to its topic. More importantly, these seven articles, taken as a whole, constitute a window through which readers may look at issues from a formal syntactic perspective and get a sense as to how work has been conducted in the framework in question, how arguments have been constructed, and how justification has been provided in the field.

The title of this book "Formal Aspects of Chinese Grammar" reflects that the articles included in the book have all used the framework of formal grammar or formal syntax, especially that of generative grammar in a broad sense. Natural languages, of course, vary from one another. However, the scope and degree of cross-linguistic variation highly restricted by a preprogrammed human language faculty believed to consist of a set of principles that are universally applicable and a set of parameters, the values of which are to be set in each particular language. A single parameter setting may result in many superficial differences between languages. Yes, it is important for linguists to work hard and figure out the rules that work specifically in each particular language and for particular structures in the language. But, even more importantly, we need to dig deep and excavate the underlying principles and parameters that, together with some basic lexical and morphological properties, are responsible for deriving those language-particular and structure-particular rules.

These articles appear largely in their original form, especially in terms of their essential contents. Revisions are minimal and mainly technical, limited to the correction of grammatical errors and clarification of expressions. Such revisions are noted in a footnote on the first page of each article, together with relevant information and full acknowledgement of its original publication details.

I would like to take this opportunity to offer my deep thanks to the Lee Foundation Singapore for a special publication grant through the Chinese and Oriental Languages Information Processing Society, and to Susanne DeVore, who proofread the whole book, page by page. Her comments and suggestions helped improve the quality of this publication. All remaining errors are solely mine.

Jie Xu
University of Macau
Macau, China
22 August 2016

Contents

Preface   v

Chapter 1
Possessor Raising in Chinese and Korean   1

Chapter 2
Two Types of Pre-Verbal Reflexives in Chinese   55

Chapter 3
The Positioning of Chinese Focus Marker *SHI* and
Pied-Piping in Logical Form   64

Chapter 4
Two Types of Null Subject Languages   89

Chapter 5
Null Object and Its Syntactic Derivation   117

Chapter 6
The Interaction of Grammatical Features
"Question" and "Focus"   140

Chapter 7
Focus-Marking in Chinese and Malay   170

References   183

Index   191

Chapter 1

Possessor Raising in Chinese and Korean[*]

ABSTRACT: *A possessor NP may move out of the Spec position of a containing NP in some Asian languages, such as Chinese and Korean, yielding the so-called "Possessor Raising Construction." From the perspective of a syntactic theory based on principles and parameters of Universal Grammar, rather than on differing sets of rules for particular languages, we argue in this chapter that the diverse Possessor Raising phenomena can well be subsumed along with "Passivization" and "Subject Raising" under the general syntactic process of "NP Movement." The movement of Possessor Raising is driven by a functional motivation, which is to separate the possessor NP from the possession NP in order to emphasize the former. It has been demonstrated that the operation of Possessor Raising is well under the constraint of UG principles in interaction with independently explainable language-particular properties, in particular, it is mainly determined by the following three factors: (1) Whether the raised possessor NP can be properly Case-marked in its new site; (2) Whether the nominal residue left behind by the NP movement can be Case-marked; and (3) Whether other applicable conditions on movement such as the Subjacency can be satisfied. Most of our arguments are constructed on the basis of the analysis of a whole set of comparable language phenomena from Chinese, Korean and English, and those phenomena, most of which are well observed in the literature, are recast and explained in a very principled way.*

---

[*]A version of this chapter originally appeared with the same title in *Languages in Contrast* 5:2 (2005), pp. 245–290. Revisions made are technical and minimal, the essential contents remain unchanged. It is included in this monograph as a chapter with kind permission from John Benjamins Publishing Company, Amsterdam/Philadelphia. [www.benjamins.com].

1.1 Introduction

A possessor NP may move out from the Spec position of a containing NP in some Asian languages, such as Chinese and Korean. This chapter starts with a brief review of the observations made in Xu (1993) and reformulates "Possessor Raising" (henceforth, PR) as a type of syntactic process (Section 1.2). From the perspective of a syntactic theory based on the principles and parameters of Universal Grammar rather than on differing sets of rules for different particular languages, in Section 1.3 we focus our attention on the question of where a raised possessor NP may move, demonstrating how the UG principles interact with independently explainable language-particular options to constrain the operation of PR cross-linguistically. Then in Section 1.4, we move on to demonstrate that whether and how PR may apply in a particular language are not only determined by whether and how the language provides a legitimate landing site for the out-raised possessor NP, but also by whether and how the Nominal residue (i.e. the possession NP) may be properly Case-marked. In Section 1.5, we proceed to examine the nature and formal properties of PR as a type of NP-Movement, especially focusing on how the Subjacency condition is satisfied in the well-formed PR-derived sentences and what role it plays in ruling out the ill-formed sentences. Also addressed is the question of what the motivations that initiate Possessor Raising are in the first place. As the discussion proceeds, relevant theoretical issues, such as V-Raising, the fundamental difference in INFL between two different types of languages, Case assignment by traces of moved verbs, Case absorption by passive morphemes, and some language-particular properties of Case systems are brought up and discussed. Our conclusions are summarized in Section 1.6.

1.2 Possessor Raising in Chinese Passive and Ergative Constructions

Xu (1993) observes that there are some interesting similarities between Chinese passive and ergative (= unaccusative) constructions with respect to the phenomena of NPs in non-Case-marked post-verbal positions. Consider the following examples.

Passive Constructions:

(1) Zhangsan bei qiang-le yibu dianshiji.
Zhangsan BEI rob-ASP one TV set
"Zhangsan was robbed of a TV set."

(2) Lisi bei bang-le yitiao tui.
Lisi BEI tie-ASP one leg
"One of Lisi's legs was tied."

Ergative Constructions:

(3) Zhangsan si-le hen.duo taoshu.
Zhangsan die-ASP many peach-tree
"Many of Zhangsan's peach trees died."

(4) Lisi chen-guo yi.tiao chuan.
Lisi sink-ASP one   ship
"One of Lisi's ships sank."

These two types of constructions are similar in several important respects:

(5) *a*. They both have NPs in the Caseless post-verbal positions;
b. The semantic relationship between the surface subject and the post-verbal NP is highly restricted in exactly the same fashion. In particular, the subject NP must be in the relationship of possessor/possession, whole/part or kinship with the post-verbal NP; and
c. The potential syntactic features of regular NPs cannot be fully realized with the post-verbal NP. The elements with definite semantic effect such as mei.yi.ge "every," zhe.ge "this" and ta.de "his/her," for instance, cannot occur in the Spec position of the post-verbal NP.

These phenomena can be properly accounted for, as Xu argues, if we adopt a PR approach as formalized in (6) below, and a modified version of Belletti's proposal on the assignment of the Partitive Case (Belletti (1988)) as in the form of (7).

(6) Possessor Raising (PR) (Xu (1993))

Move a possessor NP from a Spec/NP position to a Case-marked but non-thematic position in syntax.

(7) The Assignment of the Partitive Case

Verbs may inherently assign a Partitive Case, and its assignment carries the semantic effect of "indefiniteness" over to the Case assignees.

Note that a unified account for the two types of superficially unrelated constructions is achieved under the proposal. Although passive and ergative constructions are very much different, they are exactly analogous in failing to assign the subject position a thematic role for different reasons. Given the "Unaccusative Hypothesis" (Perlmutter 1978 and Burzio 1986),[1] the subject position of ergative verbs is intrinsically empty at the level of D-Structure. As for the passive sentences, the thematic role that is canonically assigned to the subject position is absorbed by the passive morpheme such as -en in English (Jaeggli 1986) and bei in Chinese (Xu 1993). Assuming that the surface subject NP originates from the Spec position of the object NP, (8) and (9) below are the D-Structure forms of (1) and (2) respectively.

(8) Passive Construction

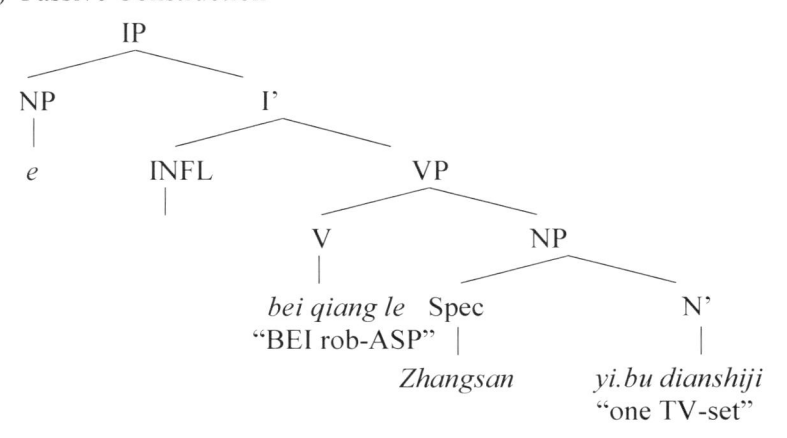

(9) Ergative Construction

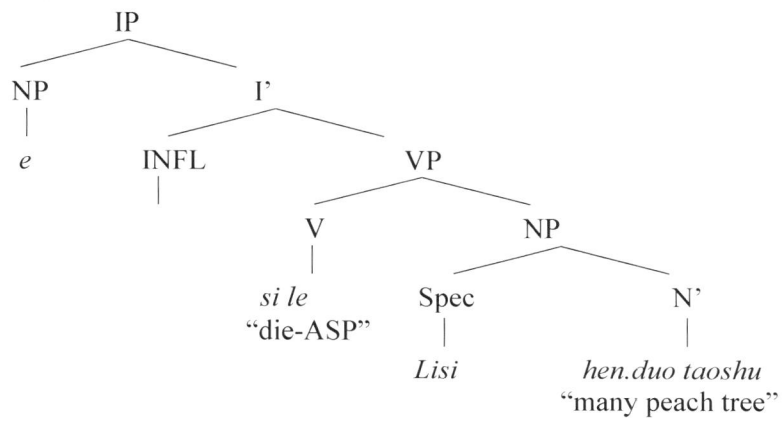

The motivation that calls for the application of the PR rule in both types of construction is exactly the same — the Case Filter. Note that sentences in the form of (8) and (9) above cannot surface since neither ergative nor passive verbs can assign the Accusative Case to the D-Structure object NPs. Two options are available which serve equally well to save the forms from the Case Filter: [1] Moving the DS object as a whole NP to the subject position, yielding (12) and (13) below (assuming that the structural particle *de* results from a later insertion); and [2] Separating the possessor NP from its head noun and moving it alone to the subject position, leaving behind the head noun, which will be eligible for the assignment of the inherent Case, the Partitive Case, yielding (1) and (3) (repeated as (10) and (11) below). As constrained by "the Indefiniteness Condition" imposed on the assignment of the Partitive, however, the whole DS object NP is not eligible for the assignment of the Partitive Case.

(10) Zhangsan$_i$ bei qiang-le t$_i$ yi.bu dianshiji.
     Zhangsan BEI rob-ASP one TV-set
     "Zhangsan was robbed of a TV set."

(11) Zhangsan$_i$ si-le t$_i$ hen.duo taoshu.
     Zhangsan die-ASP many peach-tree
     "Many of Zhangsan's peach trees died."

(12) Zhangsan de yi.bu dianshiji bei qiang-le t_i.
Zhangsan DE one TV-set BEI rob-ASP
"One of Zhangsan's TV sets was robbed."

(13) Zhangsan de hen.duo taoshu$_i$ si-le t_i.
Zhangsan DE many peach-tree die-ASP
"Many of Zhangsan's peach trees died."

It is quite clear under this analysis why the Chinese passive and ergative constructions pattern with respect to the properties listed in (5). They both fail to assign the subject position a thematic role, thus providing the out-raised NP with a legitimate landing site that meets the conditions as specified in (6) (i.e. a Case-marked but non-thematic position), so PR may apply to them. Note now that the landing site's properties of being Case-marked and non-thematic don't have to be specified as in (6). Rather, they can optimally be made to follow from the interaction of such general UG principles as the Case-Filter and the θ-Criterion: [1] The landing site has to be Case-marked since the in-moving possessor NP, like all other types of moved NPs, cannot inherit the genitive Case property of its trace and the Case-Filter requires all phonetically visible NPs to be Case-marked; [2] The new site cannot assign a new thematic role to the moved possessor NP since it, also like all other moved NPs, must inherit its thematic role from its trace (i.e. the possessor role as assigned by the head noun in an appropriate form), otherwise the θ-Criterion will be violated. Given these considerations, we propose (14) below as a simplified and generalized version of (6).

(14) Move a possessor NP out from a Spec/NP position.

1.3 Landing Site

Note that the fact that PR may apply to the Chinese passive and ergative constructions is now associated with the fact that they both have Case-marked and non-thematic positions to accommodate the out-raised possessor NP. If this approach is correct, then a natural question arises: Can a possessor NP move to somewhere other than the subject position of passive and ergative constructions if a language may serve alternative Case-marked and non-thematic landing sites? Let us approach this question by considering the properties of the Korean Double (or Multiple) Case Constructions first.

1.3.1 Korean

It is now well-known that in languages like Korean and Japanese the Accusative case may be assigned to two or more NPs in a single clause, yielding the so-called Double/Multiple Accusative Constructions. The following examples are from Korean.

(15) Mary-ka ku namwu-lul kaci-lul cal-lass-ta.
Mary-NOM the tree-ACC branch-ACC cut
"Mary cut the tree's branches/Mary cut the trees of its branches."

(16) Kay-ka   haksayng-ul tali-lul mwul-ess-ta.
dog-NOM student-ACC leg-ACC bite
"The dog bit the student's leg /
The dog bit the student on the leg."

(17) John-i   Mary-lul   elkwul-ul kuli-ess-ta.
John-NOM Mary-ACC face-ACC draw
"John has drawn Mary's face."

Since the two ACC-marked NPs in the above sentences have separate Case-markings, it is reasonable to assume that they are independent NPs at the level of S-Structure. However, one of them may be contained in the other at D-Structure, since a simple verb like mwul-ess-ta "bit" may license one and only one internal argument. Also, even at S-Structure, there is an important constraint governing this kind of double Accusative Case-marking: As Kang (1987) and O'Grady (1991) among others point out, a strict semantic relationship of "whole-part" must hold between the two ACC-marked NPs. Additionally, the second ACC-marked NP, unlike regular NPs in other positions, must be non-specific (O'Grady (1991)). To capture these language facts, we would follow Kuno (1973) and Kang

(1985) in assuming that the first ACC-marked NP designating the meaning "whole" (i.e. the possessor NP) originates from the Spec position of the second one. And we claim that PR applies here to move the possessor NP out in much the same way as the syntactic process operates on the Chinese passive/ergative constructions, as demonstrated above. However, note that Korean sentences of this type differ from the Chinese passive/ergative constructions in an important respect, that is, the latter, but not the former, have an empty subject position at DS, but the subject of the above Korean sentences are first occupied at DS as well as SS by an NP with an independent thematic role. So there are two important questions that demand an explanation from a derivational approach to the Korean double ACC-marking: [1] Where does the possessor NP move to? In other words, where is the Case-marked and non-thematic position that may serve as a legitimate landing site for an NP movement? [2] How have two NPs come to be assigned Accusative Case by a single regular (non-ditransitive) verb?

To answer these questions, we would appeal to a proposal made by Larson (1988) with regard to the VP complement in the double object construction. Details aside, one of Larson's crucial claims is that a VP may consist of an empty V (i.e. the VP shell) taking another VP as a complement. On Larson's view, the VP structure underlying the double object construction (18), for example, is postulated as (19). From their respective DS positions, the verb *send*, as required by Case assignment and Tense agreement, raises into the empty V position, and *Mary*, in order to receive Case assignment, moves to the "subject" position of the complement VP in a form that Larson identifies with Passivization.

(18) John sent Mary a letter. (Larson (1988:25))

(19)

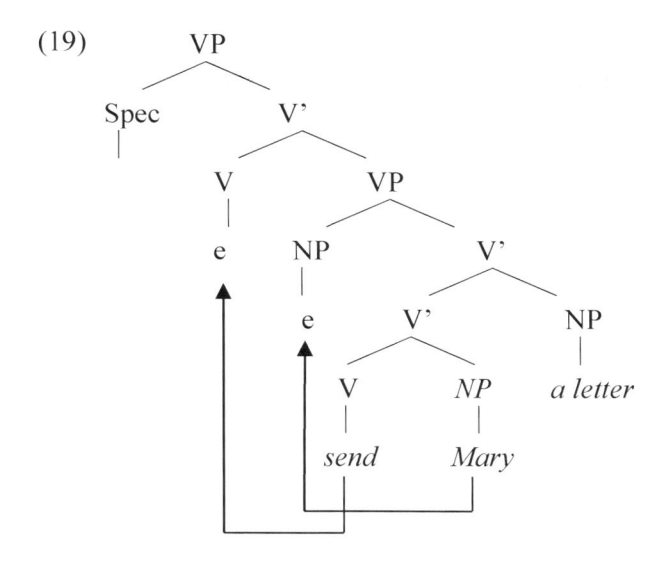

As for the Case assignment to the two object NPs, Larson proposes that two Objective (=Accusative) Cases — one structural and one inherent — can be assigned quite generally in all transitive structures, and that the double object construction is simply an instance where the two Cases are "pulled apart" and assigned to different arguments. Under this view, the raised NP *Mary* in (19) is governed by the raised V and it takes up the Specifier position of a maximal projection (i.e. the complement VP) as a sister to the raised V so that it receives a structural Objective Case from V.[2] *A letter* is assigned the inherent Objective Case by the V" which inherits the Case-assigning properties of its head (i.e. the raised V) and has undergone a V" Reanalysis in the form "[v" *t e*] -> V" (where *t* is the trace of the raised V and *e* is the trace of the moved NP).

If this analysis is correct, there is no reason that the VP structure that Larson proposes for the double object construction would be limited to that particular construction. This suggests that it is an option available generally to different types of construction, including the above Korean sentences with regular transitive verbs. If so, a simple answer to question [1] above is readily available: We may say that the VP structure underlying sentences like (15), repeated as (20), is (21) (Note that Korean is an SOV language). From their respective DS positions, the possessor NP *ku namwu* raises out of its mother NP into the empty Spec position of the complement VP, and the verb *cal*, as to assign Case to the raised NP and to satisfy the agreement requirement, moves to the empty V position, yielding the surface form.

(20) Mary-ka ku namwu-lul kaci-lul cal-lass-ta.
        Mary-NOM the tree-ACC branch-ACC cut
        "Mary cut the tree's branches/Mary cut the trees of their branches."

(21)

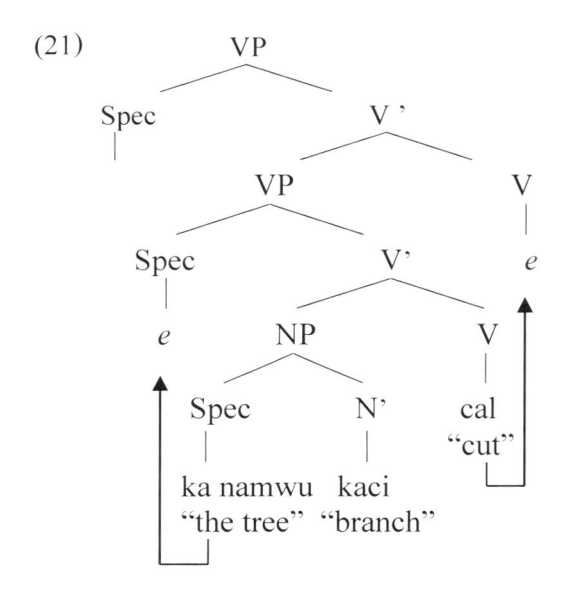

Answering question [2], departing from Larson, we would claim that the two Accusative Cases involved in the Korean Double Accusative construction are both structural: one is assigned by the raised V itself to the first ACC-marked NP; the other to the second ACC-marked NP by the trace of the raised V, which does not have to undergo Larson's V'' Reanalysis. Given the possible recursiveness of the VP complement and that the V may move successively, there is no formal syntactic limit on the number of ACC-marked NPs in a single sentence. Interestingly, the Korean language does have sentences which, as predicted, have three or more ACC-marked NPs. Diagram (23) below illustrates the derivation of a triple Accusative construction (22)

(22) Mary-ka namwu-lul seys-ul kaci-lul cal-lass-ta.
      Mary-NOM tree-ACC three-ACC branch-ACC cut
      "Mary cut three trees" branches."
      (O'Grady (1991))

(23)

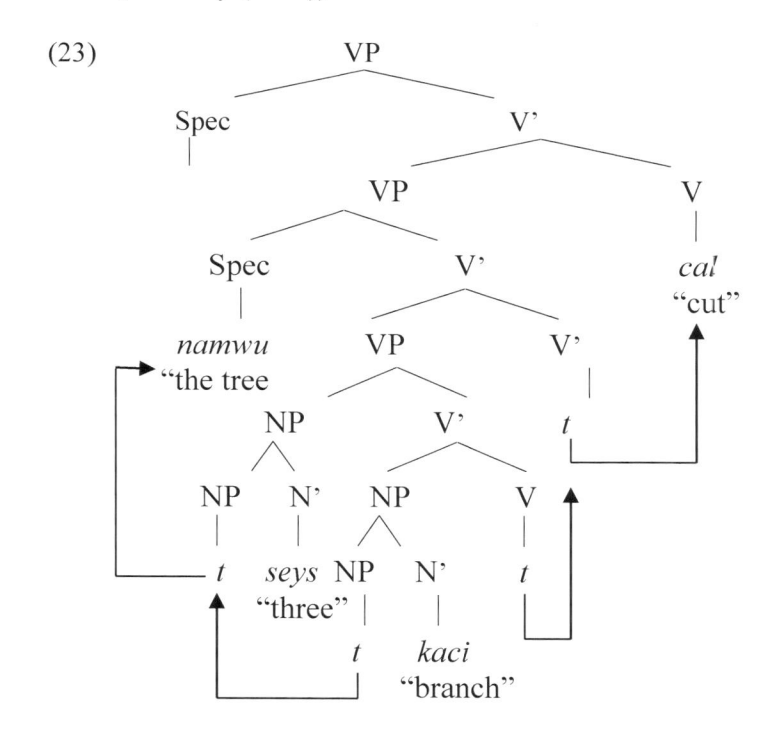

Adopting the Larson proposal about the VP complement, our account for Case assignments in the Korean multiple Accusative construction differs from Larson's account for Case assignments in the English double object construction in some nontrivial Aspects: [1] According to our analysis, the trace of a raised verb may inherit the Case-assigning property from its antecedent; [2] Consequently, only structural Accusative Case is necessary, there is no need to introduce the inherent Accusative Case;[3] and [3] There is no connection between the Case-assigning capacity of a verb and its government by INFL, and a verb or its trace may assign the structural Accusative Case regardless of whether it is governed by INFL (see also note 3). The structural Accusative Case is assigned directly and solely by the verb. One effect resulting from these differences is that, whereas Larson's account permits maximally two ACC-marked NPs (i.e. one structural and one inherent), ours allows an unlimited number of such NPs. Empirically, our proposal is more reasonable as three or more NPs may be ACC-marked in languages like Korean. As the current discussion proceeds, more arguments will be provided to show that the proposal about Case assignment by verbal trace can be generalized to handle various cross-linguistic phenomena. We will return to this issue in Sections 1.3.2, 1.3.3 and 1.4.2. At this point, we assume (24) below as a working hypothesis.

(24) A trace of a moved verb inherits the Case-assigning properties from its antecedent and may assign the Case inherited to another NP.

Under the above analysis, the Korean Double Accusative construction can be treated as with the English double object construction in terms of Case assignment to the ACC-marked NPs. This proposal seems quite reasonable, conceptually. *Kaci* "branch" in (21), for instance, is assigned the structural Accusative Case by the trace of a raised verb in much the same way a typical object NP does in a regular transitive construction. The out-raised possessor NP *ku namwu* "the tree" is governed by the out-raised V and takes up the Specifier of a maximal projection (i.e. the complement VP), which is a sister to a Case-assigning verb, so that it also receives the assignment of a structural Accusative Case from the verb itself.[4] So, our PR approach with (24) introduced, adopting Larson's VP complement proposal, provides a natural and principled account for the Korean multiple Accusative marking phenomenon.[5]

1.3.2 Chinese Again

As demonstrated in Section 1.2 above, PR may apply in Chinese to move a possessor NP to a Case-marked and non-thematic subject position in passive and ergative constructions. Given that this supposedly universal syntactic process may also function to move a possessor NP to a Spec position of a complement VP in languages like Korean, a natural question to ask is whether a possessor NP may also be moved into the Spec position of a complement VP in Chinese. The ungrammaticality of (25a) and (26a) below, in contrast with the acceptable (25b) and (26b), appears to suggest that the answer to this question is no.

(25) a. *Gou yao-le na.ge xuesheng tui.
dog bite-ASP that student leg

b. Gou yao-le na.ge xuesheng de tui.
dog bite-ASP that student DE leg
"A dog bit the student's leg."

(26) a. *Zhangsan hua Lisi lian.
Zhangsan draw Lisi face

b. Zhangsan hua Lisi de lian.
Zhangsan draw Lisi DE face
"Zhangsan drew Lisi's face."

Formally speaking, the sentences under (a) and those under (b) contrast only in the presence of the structural particle *DE*, which is generally believed to represent a kind of Genitive marking in Chinese. *DE* may be optional under certain conditions (e.g. if the Genitive NP is a pronoun like *wo* "I/me/my" in *wo(de) fuqin* "my father"). However, it is obligatory in most cases, including in (25) and (26) above where a possessor NP is placed in the Spec (Genitive) position. The absence of this structural particle in the ungrammatical sentences under (a) suggests that the possessor NPs have moved out. Quite clearly, the question is not why the sentences under (b) with the possessor NPs in the Spec are good. Rather, it is why the sentences under (a) with the possessor NPs moved out, unlike their corresponding Korean counterparts, i.e. (16) and (17) above, are bad. Given what we have been assuming for Korean, the reasonable D-Structure and derivational process for the VP of sentence (25a) should be (27).

(27)

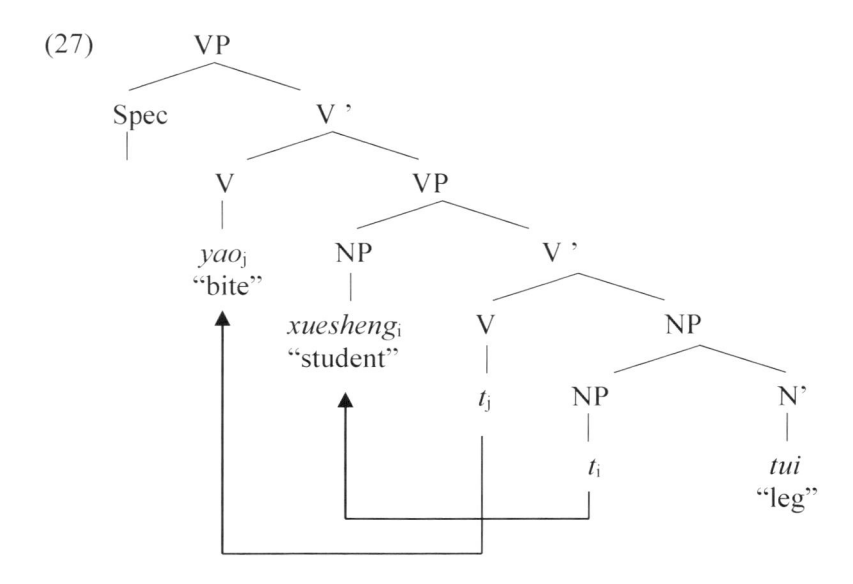

We would like to attribute the ungrammaticality of the above type of sentences to the Case Filter, in particular, to the fact that one of the two NPs involved is not properly Case-marked. Obviously, the out-raised possessor NP *xuesheng* "student" can receive the assignment of an Accusative Case from the raised verb itself, *yao* "bite", satisfying the Case Filter requirement. The other NP, *tui* "leg" is perhaps not properly Case-marked, as it is not accessible to the assignment of Case either by the raised verb itself (if we assume that the Adjacency Condition strictly holds on the assignment of Cases, and that the possessor NP intervenes between the potential Case assignor and assignee), or by the verbal trace for some unclear reason. If so, then the question now is why the verbal trace cannot inherit the Case-assigning capacities from its antecedent *yao* "bite" and assign it to *tui* "leg." In line with our current argument, we cannot simply conclude that the Chinese verbal trace, unlike its Korean counterpart, cannot assign the Accusative Case, since Chinese, like English, has double object construction as exemplified in (28) and (29) below. Also, by adopting Larson's V-Raising proposal, the well-known observation that the two NPs are assigned Accusative Case in double object constructions is made precise: they are assigned Accusative Case separately, the up-raised indirect object NP is assigned Accusative by the verb itself and the unmoved direct object by the trace of the verb.

(28) Zhangsan gei Lisi yi.ben shu.
      Zhangsan give Lisi one book
      "Zhangsan gave Lisi a book."

(29)

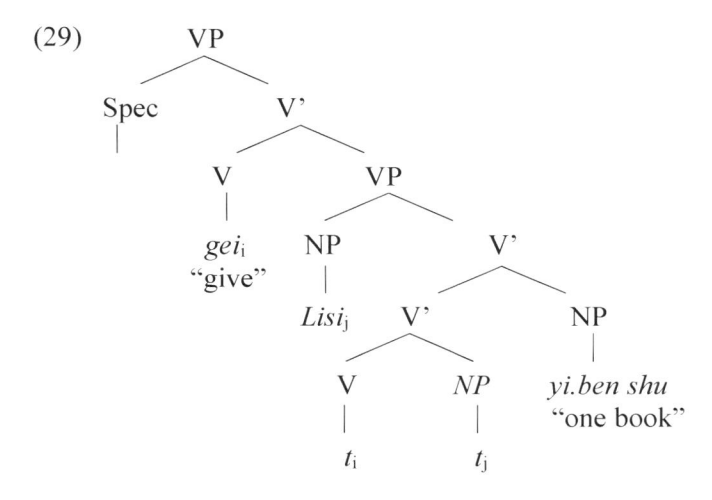

The ill-formed sentence (27) and the well-formed sentence (29) above constitute a minimal pair with respect to Case assignment by verbal traces. Also note that this sharp contrast poses a nontrivial problem for Larson (1988), who identifies regular transitive verbs with ditransitive verbs with regard to Case-assigning properties as he assumes that "quite generally in transitive structures two Objective Cases are involved — one structural and one inherent — and that the double object construction is simply an instance where the two Cases are "pulled apart" and assigned to different arguments." The obvious question is why the two Cases cannot be "pulled apart" and assigned to *xuesheng* "student" and *tui* "leg" respectively, and in particular why the inherent Case cannot be assigned to *tui* "leg".

The solution that we would like to suggest here is to place such a condition as (30) below on Case-assigning.

(30) A verb and its trace may assign the Accusative Case to separate NPs only if the verb can assign two separate thematic roles to the NPs.

If condition (30) is acceptable, then the contrast between (27) and (29) is accounted for. Sentence (29) is well-formed since its two NPs both receive assignments of the Accusative Case, one from the verb and another from the trace of the verb. Note that this is possible because the verb *gei* "give" may assign two independent thematic roles — one goal and one patient. In contrast, the two NPs in the ill-formed sentence (27) cannot receive assignments of the Accusative Case since the verb *yao* "bite" may assign only one thematic role. So, one of the two NPs in (27) is left in a Caseless position, hence the ill-formed sentence. (27) is now ruled out by (30) as a licensing condition on Case assignments. In short, the contrast in Case assignments between (27) and (29) is being naturally reattributed to the contrast in the thematic role assigning properties between the two verbs in the two sentences, and this contrast cannot be derived, but has to be specified in the lexicon.[6]

It has to be noted that (30), for unclear reasons at this point, does not hold in Korean, so in that language a verb and its trace may assign Accusative Case to two separate NPs no matter whether the verb assigns two separate thematic roles to the NPs or not. Hopefully, this cross-linguistic difference between Korean and Chinese (and English, as will be shown in 1.4.2) can be explained. We would rather leave this issue for future works.[7]

Now it should be clear why sentences under (25a) and (26a), where PR has applied, are ill-formed in Chinese. That they are ungrammatical, in fact, has nothing to do with the operation of PR itself, rather it is because some of the NPs in the resulting configurations cannot be properly Case-marked. However, as Thompson (1973), Huang (1982), and Li (1985) among others observe, Chinese has such sentences as follows.

(31) Ta ba wu.ge pingguo chidiao-le liang.ge. (Huang (1982))
      he BA five apple   eat-ASP   two
      "He ate two of the five apples."

(32) Ta ba juzi bo-le pi.
      he BA orange peel-ASP skin
      "He peeled the orange."

(33) ?Wo ba ta sha-le fuqin. (Li (1985))[8]
     I BA him kill-ASP father
     "I killed his father (and he was affected by the event adversely)."

This is one type of "*BA*-Construction" in the Chinese language. As it is widely assumed, the preposition *BA* helps move the logical object of a regular transitive structure or one of the two logical objects of a ditransitive structure from a post-verbal position to a pre-verbal position as demonstrated in (34) and (35) respectively.

(34) a. Zhangsan chi-le na.ge pingguo.
       Zhangsan eat-ASP that apple
       "Zhangsan ate that apple."

     b. Zhangsan ba na.ge pingguo$_i$ chi-le t$_i$.
       Zhangsan BA that apple   eat-ASP
       "Zhangsan ate that apple."

(35) a. Zhangsan jiegei-le Lisi yi.ben zidian.
       Zhangsan lend-ASP Lisi one dictionary
       "Zhangsan lent Lisi one dictionary."

     b. Zhangsan ba yi.ben zidian$_i$ jiegei-le Lisi t$_i$.
       Zhangsan BA one dictionary lend-ASP Lisi
       "Zhangsan lent Lisi one dictionary."

What is most remarkable about the sentences in (31)–(33) is that they are like the ditransitive construction (28) in having an NP in a post-verbal position, but they are unlike (28) in having a verb that can license only one internal thematic role. More interestingly, the possessor-possession relationship holds between the *BA* NP and the post-verbal NP in the sense now familiar to us. Also, the post-verbal NP generally has to be indefinite (non-specific). Under the PR theory developed above, it is natural to assume that these sentences arise from the application of PR. And the possessor NP (i.e. the *BA* NP) originates in the Spec of the object NP and moves up from there. (36) below, therefore, can be taken as a reasonable D-Structure representation of (32). The arrow lines indicate derivational processes.

(36)

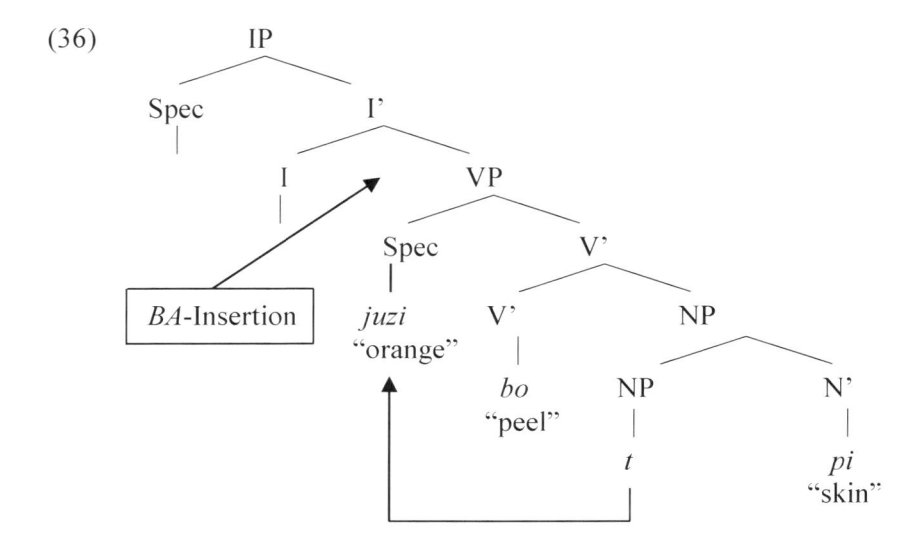

Note that in the configuration (36) where PR has applied, *pi* "skin" cannot be assigned the Accusative Case by the trace of the raised verb *bo* "peel" for reasons provided above. However, since the possessor NP *juzi* "orange" has raised out, the possession NP *pi* "skin" is now adjacent to the verb *bo* "peel" (assuming that the trace in between does not affect the adjacency), *pi* "skin" thus may be assigned the inherent Partitive Case by the verb itself. The problem is that the possessor NP *juzi* "orange" moves up and terminates in a Caseless position, since verbs generally may assign Accusative Case only to NPs to their right and the possessor NP *juzi* "orange" now is to the left of the verb. Also, note that the verb *bo* "peel" cannot raise into a higher empty V position to govern and Case-mark the possessor NP *juzi* "orange" or the possession NP *pi* "skin", depending upon the verb for the assignment of a Partitive Case, will be left Caseless. To save the sentence, especially the possessor NP in the sentence, from a potential violation of the Case Filter, the preposition *ba* is inserted before it, yielding sentences like those in (31–33). So in this sense we can say that the function of *ba* is just to serve as Case assignor, being inserted there to license an NP in the position (Huang (1982)).

It is also important to point out that the preposition *BA* can be inserted only in certain contexts, and that BA is not a mere Case assignor. Rather,

BA has a concrete meaning, making a concrete semantic contribution to the interpretation of the sentence, and the semantic effect is usually described as "disposal" in the literature (e.g. Li and Thompson (1981) among others), roughly meaning "doing something affecting the NP." So, as a lexical effect, BA may be used as a means of Case-marking only if its semantic property is compatible with the verb with which it co-occurs. In the sentences provided below, (38), which is in sharp contrast with (37), is unacceptable since the out-raised NP *Lisi* is Caseless, for reasons given above. Interestingly, sentence (38), which has an insertion of the preposition *BA*, is still ungrammatical. The reason, we may say, is that the semantics of the verb *renshi* "know" is incompatible with that of the "disposal" preposition, the insertion of *BA* creates a semantic conflict after solving a Case marking problem.[9]

(37) Zhangsan renshi-le Lisi de fuqin.
Zhangsan know-ASP Lisi DE father
"Zhangsan knows Lisi's father."
[With the structural particle *DE* indicating the possessor NP *Lisi* in its D-Structure Spec position]

(38) *Zhangsan renshi-le Lisi fuqin.
Zhangsan know-ASP Lisi father
Intended meaning: "Zhangsan knows Lisi's father."
[Without *DE*]

(39) *Zhangsan ba Lisi renshi-le fuqin.
Zhangsan BA Lisi know-ASP father
Intended meaning: "Zhangsan knows Lisi's father."
[With the insertion of *BA*]

The nature of the Chinese preposition *BA* has drawn attention from many Chinese linguists. An explanation which has been formulated in the framework that we have adopted for this study can be found in Huang (1982), where he claims that *BA* in those sentences as provided above is an inserted Case assignor. This is reasonable. However, upon further re-examination of the issue, we note that the problem may be more complicated than it appears. For example, in a sentence like (40) below, where the possessor NP *Zhangsan* has raised out (NP-raising is evidenced by the absence of *DE*), an insertion of the preposition BA still cannot save the Caseless possessor NP *Zhangsan* from a Case-Filter violation, although the semantic condition of "disposal" is satisfied there.

(40) *Ba Zhangsan fuqin bei sha-le.
        BA Zhangsan father BEI kill-ASP
        Intended meaning: "Zhangsan's father was killed"

Also note that in sentence (32), repeated below as (41), where the possession NP *pi* 'skin' is presumably assigned the inherent Partitive Case by the verb *bo* "peel", the structural Accusative Case of the same verb may not be assigned to any NP other than the NP after *BA*.

(41) Ta ba juzi bo-le pi.
        he BA orange peel-ASP skin
        "He peeled the orange."

Given these considerations, we would propose a different explanation of the nature of the preposition *BA*. Rather than saying that it is simply inserted to save an NP from a Case-Filter violation, we propose that the Accusative Case is still assigned by the verb. To satisfy the Left-to-Right condition on the assignment of Accusative Case, the preposition *BA* is inserted before the Case assignee to "host" or "transfer" the assignment. If so, we can say that the verb's potential capacity of assigning the Accusative Case is still discharged to the possessor NP *juzi* "orange" in (41) indirectly with the help of the preposition *BA* as a host. In contrast, the reason *BA*-insertion is impossible in (40) is simply because there is no Accusative Case in the first place that *BA* can help transfer to *Zhangsan*.

1.3.3 Raising a Possessor NP out of a Subject NP

We have so far identified two types of Possessor Raising: one which is observed in Chinese and which functions to move a possessor NP out of an object NP into a Case-marked and non-thematic subject position of a passive or ergative sentence (Section 1.2); and another which is observed in both Chinese and Korean, and which moves a possessor NP also out of an object NP but into a Spec position of a complement VP, with or without an accompanying insertion of a Case-assigning preposition like the Chinese *BA*. Note that the out-raised possessor NP originates from the Spec of an object position in both types of Possessor Raising. Now a natural question arises: Can the PR rule apply to move a possessor out of a subject NP? Although nothing in principle prevents such a logical possibility, the obvious question one might ask is where the possessor NP originating from the Spec of the subject NP can move to, under the constraints of UG principles, such as the locality conditions and the ECP. Given that the subject position is the most prominent position in a sentence, a downward movement of possessor NPs will leave a trace that is not properly governed, and an upward movement may violate a locality condition. But consider the following sentences from Chinese.

(42) Zhei.ke shu yezi hen da. (Li and Thompson (1981))
       this tree leaf very big
       "This tree's leaves are very big/
       This tree, (its) leaves are very big."

(43) Xiang bizi chang.
       elephant nose long
       "Elephants' noses are long/Elephants have long noses."

(44) Zhangsan fangzi hen piaoliang.
       Zhangsan house very beautiful
       "Zhangsan, (his) house is very beautiful/
       Zhangsan has a very beautiful house."

In the literature, these sentences are called either "Topic Constructions" in the sense that the sentence-initial NPs are the topics of the sentences (Li and Thompson (1981), Xu and Langendoen (1985) among others), or "Double-Subject Sentences" (i.e. Outer/Inner-Subjects) (e.g. Xing (1981)). As is noted by some authors, an interesting feature of this type of sentence is that they all have two NPs, one of which is semantically the possessor of the other. Since there is no structural particle *DE* inserted between the two NPs, the first NP must be somewhere outside of the second NP. If there is a pronoun in the Spec of the second NP, the pronoun must be co-referential with the first NP. Given these facts, we believe it is reasonable to assume that the first NP originates from the Spec of the second one and then from there it moves up to somewhere. The trace left behind may be rewritten as a resumptive pronoun.

(43') Xiang$_i$ t$_i$ bizi chang.
       elephant nose long
       "Elephants' noses are long."

(44') Zhangsan$_i$ ta$_i$ de fangzi hen piaoliang.
       Zhangsan his DE house very beautiful
       "Zhangsan, his house is very beautiful."

More interestingly, the Korean counterparts of the two pre-verbal NPs in the above sentences are both Nominative-marked, constituting the so-called "Double Nominative Constructions" as exemplified below.

(45) Mary-ka tali-ka kay-eyuyhayse mwul-li-essta. (O'Grady (1991))
      Mary-NOM leg-NOM dog-by bite-Pass
      "Mary's leg was bitten by the dog."

(46) Mary-ka elkwul-i yeyppu-ta.
      Mary-NOM face-NOM pretty
      "Mary is pretty in the face/Mary's face is pretty."

As noted in Kang (1987) and O'Grady (1991), the whole-part relationship also holds between the two Nominative-marked NPs in the same sense it does in the double Accusative constructions discussed above. To us, this strongly suggests that the first NP originates from the Spec of the second NP and from there it receives its thematic role assignment. Now the challenge again is where the first NP terminates. To tackle this problem, we would like to appeal to a parametric theory about the nature of INFL as developed in Xu (2003).

It has been proposed in Xu (2003) that the nature of INFL in Chinese-type languages (such as Japanese, Korean, etc.) is fundamentally different from that in English-type languages (also included are French and German etc.), and the difference follows from the setting of a two-valued parameter, the INFL parameter. If the parameter is fixed in the English way, it will contain the three elements [Tense] [Agr] and [Predicator]. If it is set in the Chinese way, it has only the phonetically null functional category [Predicator] as its content. It is demonstrated in Xu (2003) that the setting of this single parameter may result in enormous cross-linguistic contrasts.[10] For instance, different INFLs impose different restrictions on what can be their complements through head-complement selection. In English-type languages, only VPs can be selected as the complements of INFL since the INFL's features [Tense/Agr] have to be properly supported and since what may serve to support those features can only be verbs. Contrastively, in Chinese-type languages whose INFL contains the feature element [Predicator] only and does not have the features [Tense/Agr], a much wider variety of categories can be the complements of INFL. In Chinese, Japanese and Korean, a phrasal category can be a complement of INFL if and only if it has the feature [+Predicative].[11] So in those languages, AP, NP, PP and IP can take the complement position of INFL. What is crucial here is that the IP structure in Chinese, Japanese and Korean is recursive since IP itself can be a complement of a higher INFL. Under this analysis, in those sentences with two or more NPs in a pre-verbal position, the outer NP is the subject of the matrix IP while the inner one is the subject of the embedded IP. If so, the outer NP in the Chinese sentence (42) and that in the Korean sentence (45) can be taken to have originated from the Spec of the inner NP and from there to have undergone the Possessor Raising operation.

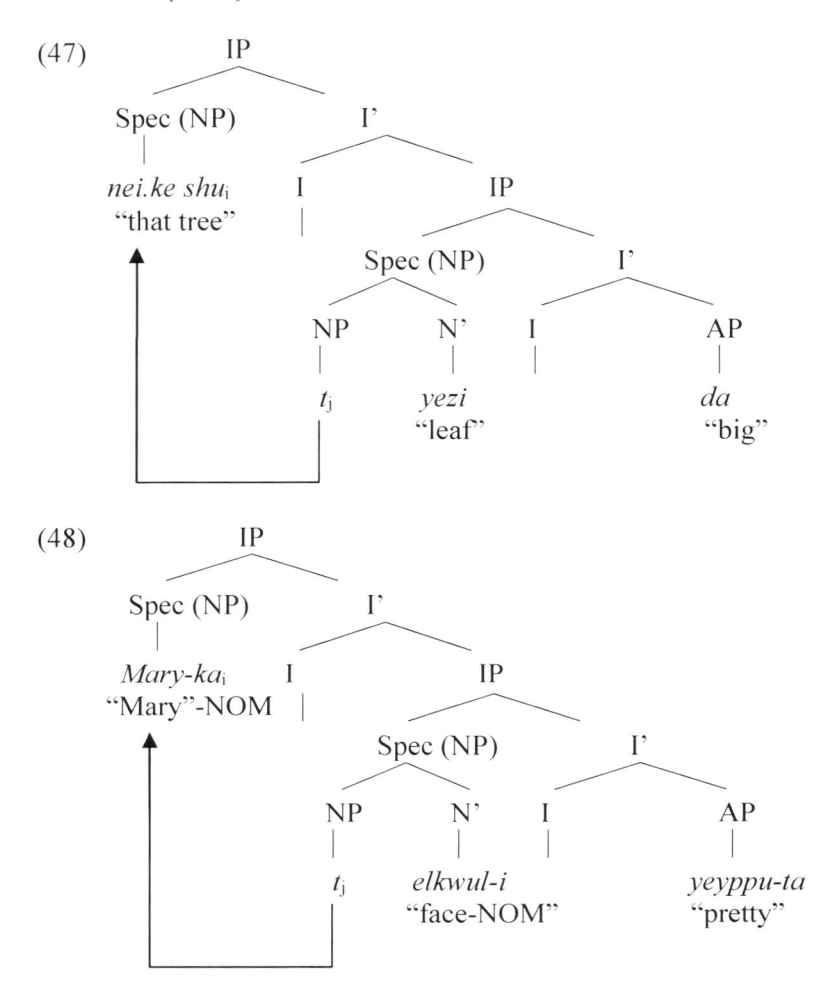

This proposal provides a natural answer to the following questions: [1] Why can two NPs be placed in "one single subject position" in Chinese? And, [2] Why can two NPs both be marked Nominative in Korean? The two NPs, regardless of whether they are overtly marked, are both assigned the Nominative Case independently by separate INFLs. Along the same lines, the well-known "Subject-/Topic-Prominent Language Typology" (Li and Thompson (1976) and (1981)) is also recast as an effect of an independently motivated parameter-setting, as argued in detail by Xu (2003). Given the unlimited recursiveness of the IP structure, there is, in principle, no formal syntactic restriction on the number of Nominative NPs that a Korean or Chinese sentence may have — although non-syntactic factors such as memory limitation, parsing principles, pragmatic considerations and so forth may limit the number in actual speech to a certain extent. (49) below serves as a good example in which four NPs are marked Nominative (example taken from O'Grady (1991)), and (50) illustrates how such a sentence is derived.

(49) Mary-ka elkwul-i kho-ka olun-ccok-i yeyppu-ta.
     Mary-NOM face-NOM nose-NOM right-side-NOM pretty
     "Mary is pretty in the face on the nose on the right side."

(50)

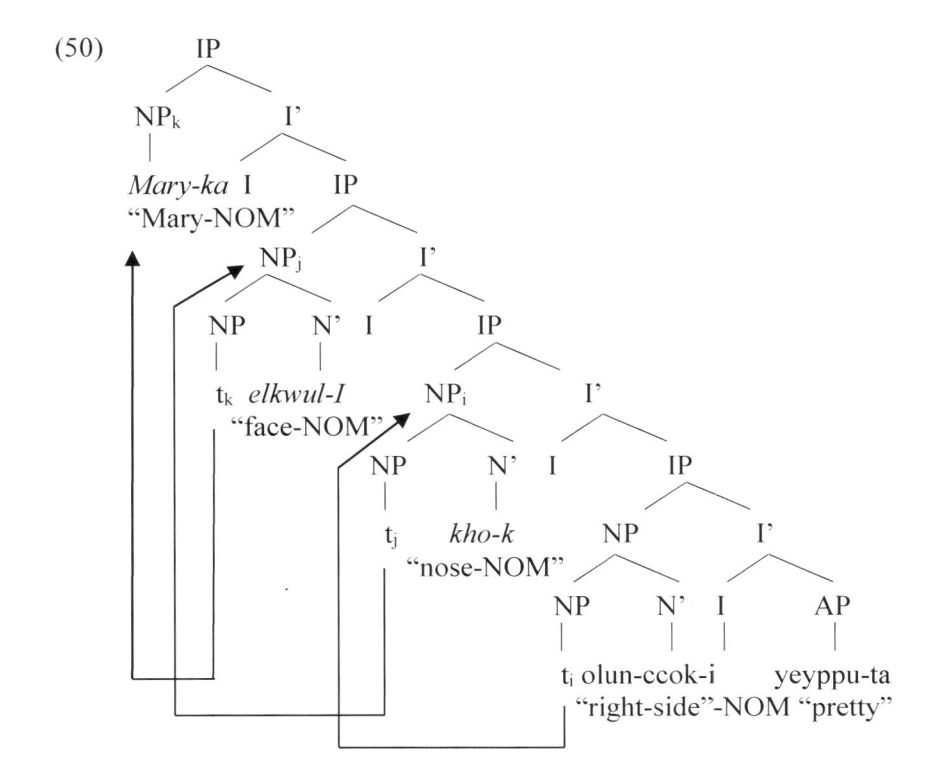

There are two potential problems for this analysis: [1] As the landing sites for those out-raised possessor NPs, are the outer NP positions (i.e. the higher subject positions) assigned Cases and/or thematic roles? If the answer is yes, then how? [2] Is the Subjacency Condition observed in the course of movement? As for question [1], please recall that the potential landing sites for incoming possessor NPs have to be Case-marked and non-thematic, as an effect of the interaction of the Case-Filter and θ-Criterion. Note that there is no problem with the Case-marking of the positions if we adopt Xu's proposal about the INFL parameter. Those positions are assigned the Nominative Case by separate INFLs just as any other typical subject positions would be (Xu (2003)). As for the thematic roles of those positions, we follow Lebeaux (1983) in assuming that the outer NP positions (or "Topic positions" in Lebeaux and many other authors' terminology) are "non-thematic positions" in the sense that they are not assigned thematic roles either by an IP, by a VP, or by a V. Their semantic relationship to the lower IPs is "aboutness" in some loose sense. In short, the outer subject positions are well qualified as landing sites for possessor NPs to move to.

The Subjacency Condition, in its standard version, can also be observed in the derivational process based on the simple and natural assumption that Chinese and Korean have CP (= S') rather than IP (=S) as the bounding node along with NP. Although in languages like Chinese it may not be that easy to distinguish IP from CP technically since those languages have neither overt *Wh*-movement nor a lexical Complementizer such as English "that," the IP status of the lower clause can be observed due to the fact that it cannot have an independent *Wh* feature. So, the out-raising possessor NP crosses only one bounding node — an NP node — at each step of movement, which satisfies the Subjacency Condition. Of course, the possessor NP, just like any other kind of NP, may move cyclically.

It should be pointed out that the above analysis of some sentences with double-subjects in Chinese and those with double-Nominatives in Korean, as derived through the application of PR, does not require that all NPs in the outer subject position are placed there through the operation of PR. In fact, the NP may well be base-generated there and remain there, yielding what Cole, Hermon and Sung (1990) call "Non-gap topic construction" as exemplified in (51) and (52) below. Even if it is movement-created, it may also originate from the object position of an inner IP as is seen in (53).

(51) Shuiguo wo xihuan pingguo. (Cole, Hermon and Sung (1990))
     Fruit   I   like   apple
     "As for fruits, I like apples."

(52) Zhei ban xuesheng ta zui congming. (Li and Thompson (1981))
     this class student   he most intelligent
     "(In) this class of students, he is the most intelligent."

(53) Nei.ge bowuguan$_i$ wo yijing canguan-le t$_i$.
     that museum I already visit-ASP
     "I have already visited that museum."

1.3.4 Korean Again: Alternations in Case-marking

Since a possessor NP may either stay in its D-Structure position where it is Case-marked Genitive, or move out to another position where it is Case-marked differently, there are alternations in NPs' Case-marking between Genitive and other Cases such as Accusative and Nominative. That is, a certain NP can be marked Genitive in one sentence and Accusative in another sentence without substantial change in the basic semantics. This is a widely noted phenomenon in languages like Korean (e.g. Choi (1988), and O'Grady (1991) among others). This phenomenon turns to be more interesting and more intricate in interaction with passivization, since the latter normally affects Case-marking in many languages (e.g. Korean). This kind of complication in Case-marking has drawn wide attention in the field.[12]

Rather than taking readers through those proposals, here we shall demonstrate how the phenomenon can be accounted for in a more economical and more principled way under the theory that we have been developing here. What is expected here is that the phenomenon can be made to follow from independently motivated principles with no extra stipulations. Consider the following sentences [once again, examples taken from O'Grady (1991)].

(54) Mary-ka ipalsa-eyuyhayse meli-lul/ka cal-li-ess-ta.
      Mary-NOM barber-by hair-ACC/-NOM cut-Pass
      "Mary was cut the hair by the barber."

(55) Kim yang-i John-eyuyhayse son-ul/-i cap-hi-ess-ta.
      Kim Miss-NOM John-by hand-ACC/-NOM hold-Pass
      "Miss Kim was held by the hand by John."

Meli "hair" in (54) above, for example, may be marked either Accusative
or Nominative. In our opinion, the difference in Case-marking results
from different derivational processes. In particular, the above alternation
in Case-marking is determined by whether the two relevant processes —
Passivization and Possessor Raising — apply, and how they apply in the
derivations. (56) below is the corresponding derivation for the sentence in
which *meli* "hair" has an Accusative marking, and (57) for the sentence
with the very same word marked Nominative.

(56)

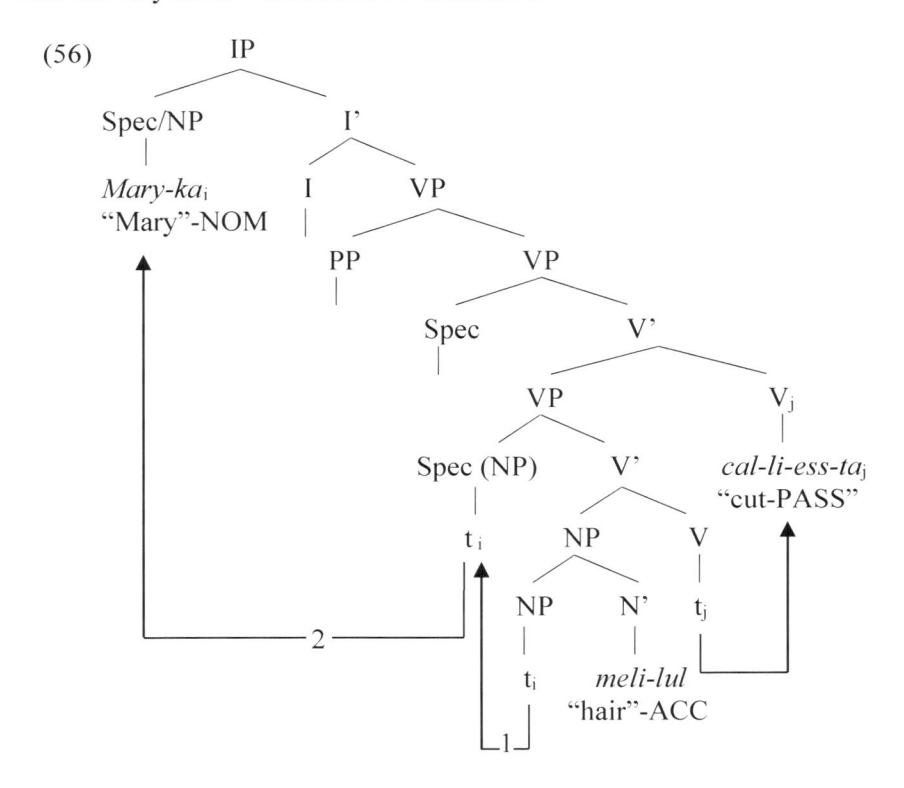

(57)

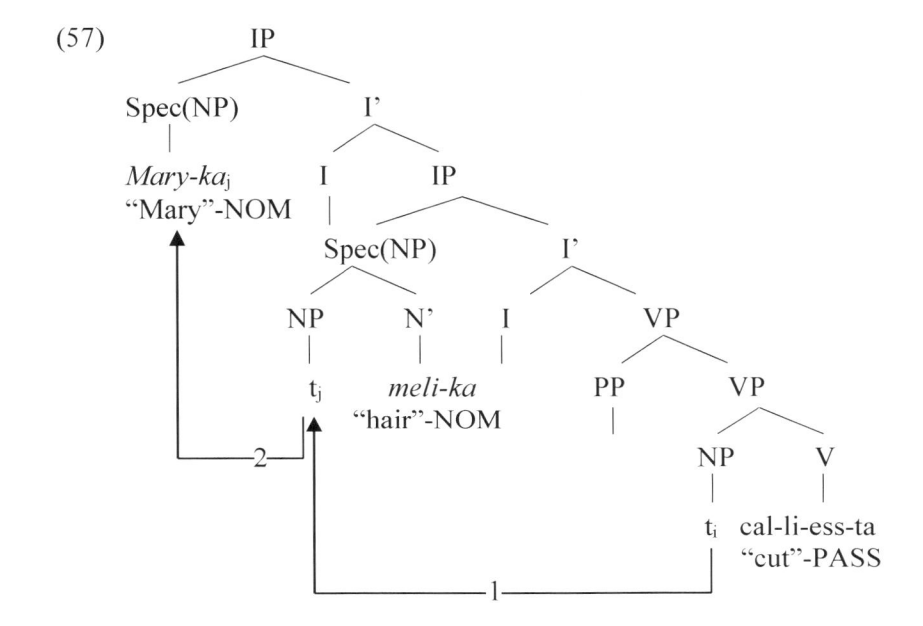

Note that the two derivational processes are different: In (56), PR has first applied to move the possessor NP *Mary* into the Spec of a complement VP (i.e. Step 1), then the Passivization applies to move the same NP into the subject position of the sentence (Step 2). The possession NP *meli* "hair" is assigned the Accusative Case by the trace of an up-raised verb based on the natural assumption that the Case absorption by the passive morpheme takes away only the Case-assigning capacity of the morpheme-carrying verb without affecting the Case-assigning property of its trace. But the possessor NP *Mary*, which counts on the passivized verb for Case assignment, has to move away. In this particular case, it moves to the subject position whereby it is assigned a Nominative Case. In derivation (57), by contrast, the Passivization has applied before PR does; the V-Raising thus is not motivated and there is no verbal trace. The passivized verb's Case capacity is absorbed by the passive morpheme, and consequently the whole NP moved into the lower subject position first (Step 1), then PR applied to raise the possessor NP alone into the higher subject position. The possessor and possession NPs are each assigned a Nominative Case by an independent INFL. The above alternation in Case-marking is thus naturally derived.

Based on the standard assumption about the Case-assigning property of passivized verbs, NPs governed by passivized verbs cannot be assigned the Accusative Case, since the morphology of the passivized verbs somehow "absorbs" Case (Chomsky (1981)). Taking this a step further, Jaeggli (1986) attributes the loss of the Case-assigning capacity of passivized verbs to absorption by the passive morpheme (e.g. *en* in English), and this property of passive morphemes perhaps should be specified in the lexicon, which accommodates all kinds of related irregularities. However, it has to be pointed out that passivized verbs in Chinese are still capable of assigning the inherent Partitive Case, although they are not capable of assigning the structural Accusative Case as illustrated in Section 2. For us, this phenomenon suggests clearly that the passive morpheme's Case absorption affects the structural Accusative Case only but not the inherent Partitive Case. Even more interestingly, as is seen in some examples from the Korean language in which verbs and their traces may assign Accusative Case to separate NPs no matter what the thematic role-assigning capacity of the verbs is, passivized verbs are also capable of assigning the Accusative Case, which suggests that the passive morpheme's Case absorption probably takes away one and only one Accusative Case, leaving the passivized verb's Case-assigning capacity, if any, largely unaffected. Moreover, adopting Larson's V-Raising proposal, we can make it clear how the multiple Accusative Case assignments are done in double object constructions, perhaps in all languages, and in regular transitive constructions in such languages as Korean: The Accusative Case is assigned to two or more NPs separately by the verb and its trace or traces (in this manner, the one-to-one correspondence between Case assignors and assignees is maintained, a welcome by-product). If this approach is correct, a more precise theory of Case absorption in passives becomes possible, which can be formulated roughly as in (58).

(58) The passive morpheme's Case absorption absorbs one and only one Accusative Case assigned by the lexical verb that carries the morpheme without affecting any other Case capacities of the verb and its trace.

The proposal articulated here makes predictions. It predicts, for example, that the out-moving NP in Korean passives has to be the outmost possessor NP, since it depends on the passive morpheme-carrying verb itself for Case assignment. This prediction is supported in the language. Furthermore, under (58), an interesting contrast between two types of English passive double object constructions, as presented in Larson (1988), can be more naturally accounted for. That contrast is exemplified by the pair of sentences in (59) and (60).

(59) Mary was sent a letter.

(60) ?*A letter was sent Mary.

As noted correctly in Larson (1988), sentence (59) is a perfectly well-formed one, while sentence (60) is not. Without (58), Larson has to appeal to such assumptions as that the derived direct object receives only the structural Case. Our account is much simpler. As illustrated in (61) below, the ungrammaticality of (60) can be readily attributed to an effect of the Case Filter in interaction with (58). In particular, it is because *Mary* in the sentence is not properly assigned Case in a post-verbal position. First, the passivized verb *sent* itself is deprived of Case-assigning capacity by the passive morpheme and thus is unable to assign Accusative Case to it. Second, the trace of the verb is not structurally high enough to govern and to assign a structural Case to *Mary* although it is, in principle, capable of assigning Accusative Case to the NP. On the other hand, the two NPs in the well-formed sentence (59) are both properly Case-marked. *Mary* in the subject position is assigned Nominative case as usual, whereas *a letter* takes an assignment of Accusative Case from a verbal trace whose Case-assigning capacity is preserved and which is structurally high enough to govern and to Case-mark the NP.

*(61)

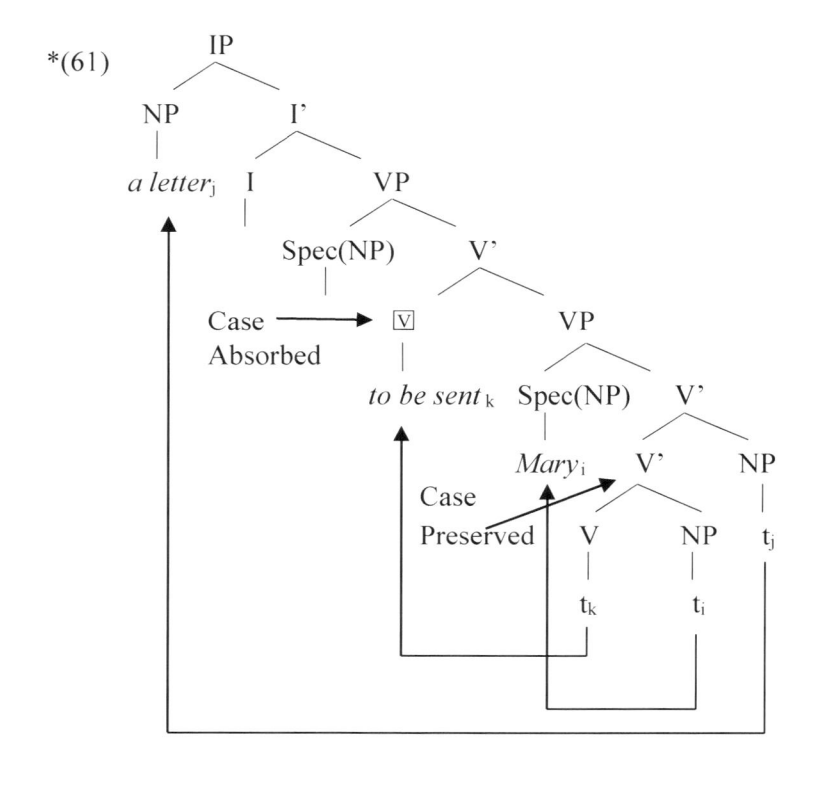

(62)

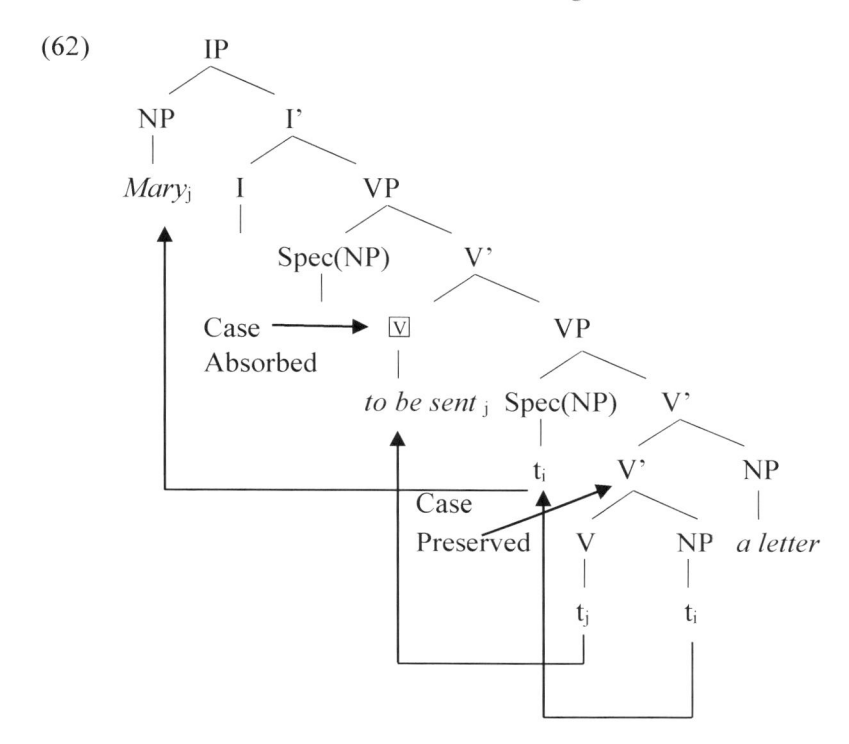

The same kind of contrast is also observed in the Chinese passive double object construction, which can be accounted for in much the same way.

(63) a. Zhangsan bei song-le yi.ben shu.
Zhangsan BEI give-ASP one book
"Zhangsan was given a book."

b. ?*Na.ben shu bei song-le Zhangsan.
that book BEI give-ASP Zhangsan
Intended meaning: "That book was given (to) Zhangsan."

(64) a. Zhangsan bei wen-guo zhe.ge wenti.
Zhangsan BEI ask-ASP this question
"Zhangsan was asked this question."

b. *Zhe.ge wenti bei wen-guo Zhangsan.
this question BEI ask-ASP Zhangsan
Intended Meaning: "*This question was asked Zhangsan."

1.4 Case Assignment to the Nominal Residue

From the preceding discussion, it should be clear at this point that a language has to provide a properly Case-marked, non-thematic landing site for an out-raising possessor NP so that PR can apply in the language. But note that there are two NPs observed at the level of S-Structure where Case-assignments are checked: the raised possessor NP and the residue of the raising movement, i.e. the possession NP, which is also the Nominal head with a trace in its Spec. In principle, these two NPs are both subject to the Case-Filter. In this section, we shall demonstrate that proper Case-marking of the possessor NP is only a necessary but not a sufficient condition for the PR operation. Whether and how the residue of the raising movement can be properly Case-marked also plays a crucial role in the syntactic operation of PR.

1.4.1 Partitive Case as an Option

It is noted in Section 1.2 above that the post-verbal possession NP in Chinese passive and ergative constructions receives the assignment of the inherent Partitive Case. Only this inherent Partitive can possibly be assigned to the NP in ergative constructions, since ergative verbs cannot assign thematic role to the subject, as Burzio's Generalization specifies. As is discussed in Section 1.3.2, the Accusative Case is simply not an option for assignment to the NP in the Chinese passive because the passive morpheme *BEI* absorbs the Case-assigning capacity of the verb itself and the trace of the verb is prohibited by condition (30) from assigning the Accusative Case. In short, the Partitive Case is the only source that this NP can count on for its Case assignment. Let us reconsider examples in (1) and (3), repeated as (65) and (66) below, respectively.

$$\nearrow \text{PARTITIVE} \searrow$$

(65) Zhangsan bei qiang-le yi.bu dianshiji. [Passive Construction]
      Zhangsan BEI rob-ASP one TV-set
      "Zhangsan was robbed of a TV set."

(66) Zhangsan si-le <u>henduo taoshu</u>.   [Ergative Construction]

         / PARTITIVE ↘

      Zhangsan die-ASP many peach-tree

      "Many of Zhangsan's peach trees died."

Given that PR phenomena are also observed in Korean, an interesting question arising at this point is whether an NP in a Korean sentence, if necessary, can be assigned the Partitive Case. First of all, since the traces of verbs in Korean in general can assign the structural Accusative Case quite freely and the passive morpheme's Case absorption does not affect the Case-assigning capacity of verbs' traces, the possession NP as a Nominal residue of PR in Korean passives is assigned the structural Accusative Case readily and thus does not need such an inherent Case in the first place, regardless of whether the Case is available in the language. The only construction in which the Partitive Case may be needed is the ergative construction. Like all other languages, Korean, of course, has ergative verbs and ergative constructions in which the S-Structure subject NP, by the now familiar hypothesis, originates from the object position in Korean, which is an SOV language. Consider the following two examples.[13]

(67) John-uy/-ka   apeci-ka$_i$ t$_i$ tolakasietta.

      John-Gen/-NOM father-NOM died

      "John's father died."

(68) Onasis-uy/-ka pay-ka$_i$ t$_i$ karaanciessta.

      Onasis-Gen/-NOM ship-NOM sunk

      "Onasis' ship sunk."

As illustrated above, the possessor NP may be marked either Genitive or Nominative. This alternation in Case-marking suggests clearly that the possessor NP may either remain in the Spec position of NP (thus marked Genitive) or be raised out to a subject position (then marked Nominative). This is against nothing we have been proposing so far. However, what is interesting here is that possession NPs, such as *apeci* "father" and *pay* "ship," can only be marked Nominative, implying that it is obligatory for them to move to subject positions. A natural question here is why the possession NPs in Korean cannot remain alone in their D-Structure positions and get assigned Partitive Case there just as their counterparts in Chinese do when the possessor NPs raise up?

(67') *John -ka$_i$ t$_i$ apeci tolakasietta.
        John-NOM father died
        Intended meaning: "John's father died."

(68') *Onasis-ka$_i$ t$_i$ pay karaanciessta.
        Onasis-NOM ship sunk
        Intended meaning: "Onasis' ship sunk."

We would attribute the ungrammaticality of (67') and (68') to the unavailability of the inherent Partitive Case in the Korean language. Note that this approach entails a nontrivial theoretical implication of Case theory; that is, some Cases (or the assignment) may be language-particular while others are universal. A language-particular Case may be available in some languages but not in others whereas universal Cases are available in all languages (e.g. Nominative Case). It is hoped that the language-particular nature of some Cases can be somehow derived from either parameter-setting or other language-particular options, such as lexical properties. In this article, we leave the question open, merely pointing out that a similar spirit is also felt in Kayne's analysis of preposition stranding. Kayne (1981) suggests that the basic property of English that makes it have preposition stranding is that those prepositions in the language don't assign Oblique Case (in our words, the Oblique Case is not available in the language), rather the English prepositions assign Objective (=Accusative) case just like verbs. This property of prepositions makes it possible for them to be thematically reanalyzed with the verb when a prepositional object is extracted, and the trace of the object, as governed by the reanalyzed V-P, is properly licensed under the ECP. On the other hand, in languages like French and Spanish where prepositions assign Oblique Case, reanalysis is blocked due to Case conflict between V as an Objective Case assignor and P as an Oblique Case assignor, hence no preposition stranding is possible in those languages.

Please note that our major claim here is that the UG only requires all phonetically visible NPs to be properly Case-marked as an effect of the Case Filter, but it does not prescribe a specific Case system for each and every particular language. The latter, we assume, is left to be determined jointly by language-particular options in accordance with other independent UG principles. Consequently, there may be some Cases which are available in some languages (e.g. the Oblique in French and Spanish, and the Partitive in Finnish and Chinese), but not in others. The diversity in morphological Case-marking observed widely in different languages, in our view, is a reflex of this theoretical possibility.

1.4.2 PR in English

As a preliminary observation, we can say that the Partitive Case is not available in English either. In English ergative constructions like (69) and (70) below, the possessor and possession NPs have to be moved together to the subject position. It is impossible for the possessor NP alone to move up into the subject position and leave the possession nominal head behind in a post-verbal position. The two sentences in (71) and (72) are ungrammatical also because the Partitive Case is not available in the language, and other than the Partitive, the post-verbal NPs *father* and *ship* have no potential Case assignment.

(69) John's father$_i$ died t$_i$.

(70) The company's ship$_i$ sank t$_i$.

(71) *John$_i$ died t$_i$ father.

(72) *The company$_i$ sank t$_i$ a ship.
      (With intended meaning not being 'a company sank a ship deliberately')

Moreover, what happens in Korean does not seem to be possible in English. Recall that the structural Accusative Case may be assigned to two or more NPs in the Korean regular transitive construction as exemplified in (15) and (16), repeated below as (73) and (74) respectively. Based on the analysis developed in this article, the left Accusative-marked NP is assigned by the verb itself, and the right one by the trace of the verb. This is impossible in English since comparable sentences like (75) and (76) below are ungrammatical.

(73) Mary-ka ku namwu-lul kaci-lul cal-lass-ta.
      Mary-NOM the tree-ACC branch-ACC cut
      "Mary cut the tree's branches/Mary cut the tree of its branches."

(74) Kay-ka haksayng-ul tali-lul mwul-ess-ta.
      dog-NOM student-ACC leg-ACC bite
      "The dog bit the student's leg/The dog bit the student on the leg."

(75) *Mary cut the tree branches.
      Intended meaning: "Mary cut the tree's branches."

(76) *The dog bit the student leg.
      Intended meaning: "The dog bit the student's leg."

Note first that the ungrammaticality of (75) and (76) in English raises an immediate question for Larson's analysis (Larson (1988)): Why can the two Accusative Cases, one inherent and the other structural, not be "pulled apart" and be assigned to *tree* and *branches* separately? More specifically, why can the inherent Accusative Case not be assigned to *branches* while the structural one is assigned to *tree*? According to our proposal, *branches* is not assigned Accusative Case simply because the Case-assigning ability of the verbal trace is subject to condition (30) in English as well as in Chinese. Condition (30) basically says that a verb and its trace may assign Accusative Case to different NPs separately only if the verb may assign thematic roles to different NPs separately. Obviously, sentences (75) and (76) don't satisfy this condition as the verbs *bite* and *cut* may each assign only one thematic role (the patient role) to one single NP.

(77)

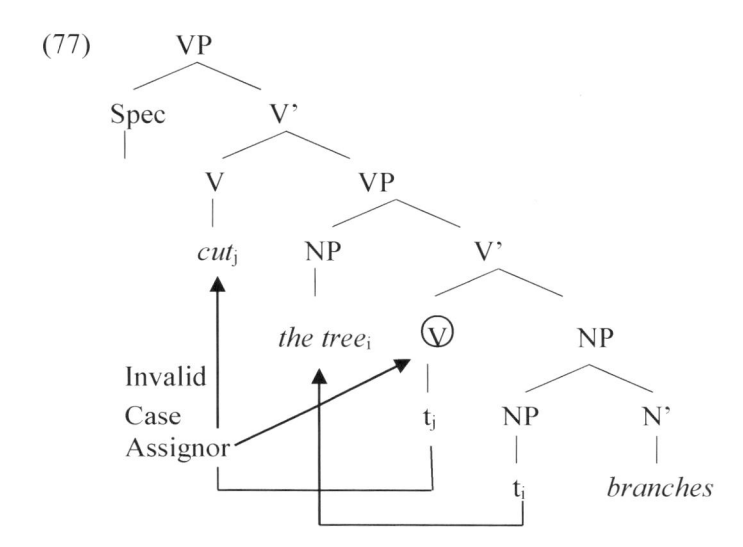

Given the above discussion, we may now generalize and say that [1] the Partitive Case is not available in English; and [2] the Case-assignment by verbal trace is subject to condition (30) in the language. And these are the reasons potential PR constructions like (71)–(72) and (75)–(76) are unacceptable in English. However, consider the following English sentences.

(78) Somebody robbed John of (his/the) money.

(79) Somebody shot Bill in his/the back.

(80) The dog bit Mary on her/the leg.

(81) John caught Bill by his/the hand.

(82) Mary punched John in the/his nose.

These sentences are remarkable at least in the following respects:

[1] Only the definite article *the* or pronouns such as *his*, *her* and *their* can occur in the Spec position of the NPs, which are prepositional objects. Proper names and full NPs such as *Bill* and *the man on the bed*, for example, cannot take up the Spec position of the NPs. Also, if a pronoun is placed in the position, it will be forced to be co-referential with the object NP. This is puzzling when one notes that the relevant Binding principle only requires

a pronoun to be free in its governing category. For the same reason, the following two sentences are unacceptable.

(83) *Somebody robbed John of Bill's money.

(84) *Somebody robbed John$_i$ of her$_i$ money.

[2] The semantic relationship between the main verb and its surface object NP in those sentences is somehow different from what is commonly observed between an action verb and its object NP. In a simple sentence like *John ate apples*, for example, the action of eating is directly imposed over the NP *apples*. By contrast, in sentence *Mary punched John in his nose*, what is being punched is not *John* as a whole person. Rather, it is only *his nose* that directly receives the action, although *John*, of course, is also somehow affected indirectly by the action operated on his nose.

[3] The post-verbal prepositional phrases in those sentences are very much different from typical English PPs in their syntactic behavior. For example, the latter, in most cases, can be moved to a sentence-initial position quite freely. But the PPs in the above sentences cannot be moved there. This is why sentences in (78')–(82') are unacceptable in contrast with (85b) and (86b), which are well-formed.

(85) a. John left California for New York <u>on the 5th of July</u>.

     b. <u>On the 5th of July</u>, John left California for New York.

(86) a. Bill painted his car <u>in the parking lot</u>.

     b. <u>In the parking lot</u>, Bill painted his car.

(78') *<u>Of (his/the) money</u>, somebody robbed John.

(79') *<u>In his/the back</u>, somebody shot Bill.

(80') *<u>On her/the leg</u>, the dog bit Mary.

(81') *<u>By his/the hand</u>, John caught Bill.

(82') *<u>In his/the nose</u>, Mary punched John.

In our interpretation, such formal properties clearly suggest a derivational account of those sentences. Specifically, they are examples of the English Possessor Raising construction, arising from the application of PR. The challenge, then, is simply how to bring the derivation within the scope of established theoretical principles and how to constrain it in an appropriate way. We here would claim that the surface prepositional object NP *the nose* in the sentence *Mary punched John in the nose* is the direct object of the verb *punch* and the surface object NP *John* originates from the Spec position of the D-Structure object NP and from there it raises into the Spec position of a complement VP. Meanwhile, V-Raising takes the verb *punch* up into a VP-shell.

(87)

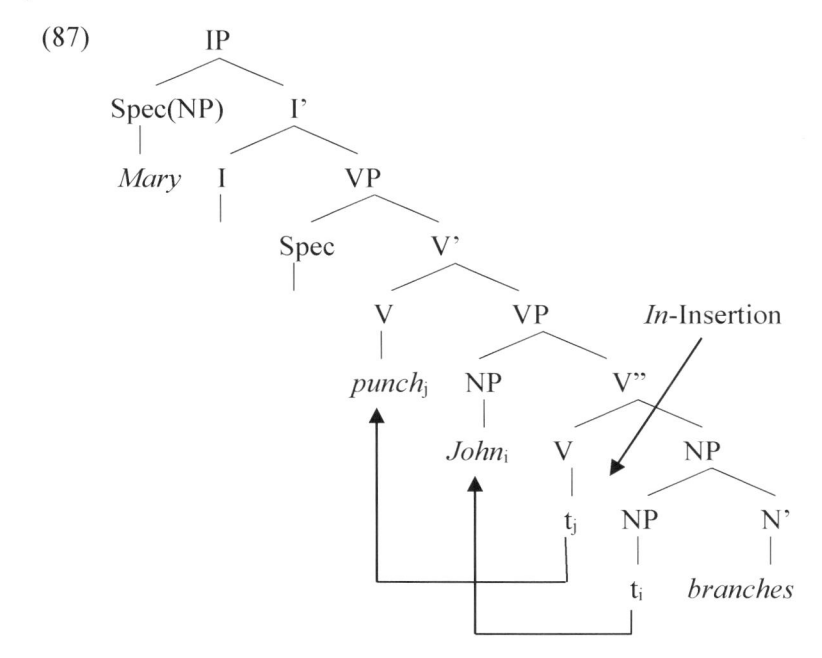

Note that the trace of the verb *punch* in the above configuration is not able to assign a Case to the residue of PR movement *nose* since condition (30) is not satisfied there. *Nose* is therefore left in a Caseless position. To save this NP from the Case Filter, the preposition *in* is inserted before it. This preposition insertion is similar to the Chinese *BA*-insertion as discussed in Section 1.3.2, the only difference is that the Chinese *BA* is inserted before a raised possessor NP, whereas the English preposition is placed before the possession NP left behind. This difference can easily be accounted for on our analysis. As noted above, *BA* in Chinese is not a Case-assigning category, rather it functions to transfer Case assignment by a verb to an NP. But it is quite clear that these two languages are analogous in employing the same device to satisfy the Case Filter, that is, inserting a preposition before a Caseless NP. Also, note that the otherwise puzzling properties of the sentences illustrated above can now be taken as expected. First, the semantic property between the main verb and its surface object NP in the relevant sentences now needs no further explanation. Second, after an application of PR, the trace of the out-raised possessor NP can optionally be rewritten as a resumptive pronoun (but not an R-expression), giving rise to sentences like *Mary punched John in his nose*. The resumptive pronoun *his*, of course, has to be co-referential with its antecedent *John*. If the resumptive pronoun option is not selected, then the definite article *the* has to be placed there for an independent reason, yielding sentences like *Mary punched John in the nose*. Third, it is an expected ECP effect that a prepositional phrase such as *in his/the nose* in sentence *Mary punched John in his/the nose*, unlike other adverbial PPs, cannot be moved to a sentence-initial position. The reason is that the prepositional object contains a trace in its Spec no matter whether spelled out as a resumptive pronoun or not, and if the prepositional phrase moves with a trace in it, the antecedent of the trace will not be able to properly govern it, hence an ECP violation. Moreover, it should also be noted that the Prepositional Phrases with the prepositions inserted rather than base-generated cannot, in general, be moved. (88) and (89) below are considered to be putative cases, which involve preposition-insertion for Case satisfaction Chomsky (1986)). Prepositional phrases in the sentences cannot be moved to sentence-initial positions either.

(88) I persuaded John of the importance of going to college.
     (= Chomsky (1986:265i))
     ≠*Of the importance of going to college, I persuaded John.

(89) John is uncertain of the time. (= Chomsky (1986:265ii))
     ≠ *Of the time, John is uncertain.

It should be pointed out that the kind of preposition insertion assumed here involves more prepositions than that noted in Chomsky (1986). For instance, we have the insertion of prepositions of *of* (78), *in* (79) and (82), *on* in (80), and *by* in (81), and probably some others. Our explanation of this matter is that formal grammar simply requires that a preposition be inserted to save a Caseless NP from violating the Case Filter, without specifying which preposition be chosen and inserted there. A choice among different prepositions, as a matter of purely lexical properties, is perhaps based on the semantic compatibility between the prepositions and the verbs with which they co-occur.

The English Possessor Raising construction such as *Mary punched John in his nose*, of course, may undergo the process of Passivization, yielding sentences like (90) below. The relevant derivational process can be diagrammed as in (91) with the irrelevant agentive PP being omitted. Note that the raised possessor NP *John* has to move further up since the Case-assigning capacity of the passivized verb *punched* has been absorbed.

(90)   John was punched by Mary in his nose.

(91)

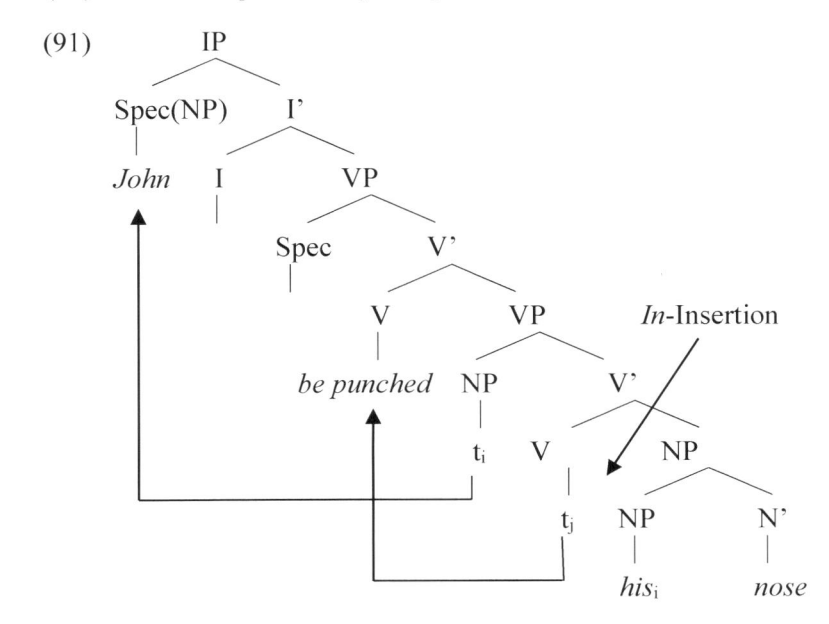

The following sentences provide further examples:

(92) John was robbed of his/the money by somebody.

(93) Bill was shot in his/the back by somebody.

(94) Mary was bitten on her/the leg by a dog.

(95) Bill was caught by his/the hand by John.

In closing this section, we would like to point out that PR operation in English is very much restricted, due to various independent language-particular reasons. In addition to what has been noted above in this article, i.e. that the Partitive Case is not available in the language, that the strict condition (30) on Case-assignment of verbal traces applies to the language, and so forth, the English setting of the INFL parameter as [Tense, Agr, Predicator] also renders a possessor NP unable to be raised out from an inner subject position into an outer one. (96) below is unacceptable in contrast with its Chinese counterpart (97), which is well-formed.

(96) *John$_i$ t$_i$ house is very beautiful.
      Intended meaning: "John's house is very beautiful."

(97) Zhangsan$_i$ t$_i$ fangzi hen piaoliang.
      Zhangsan   house very beautiful
      "Zhangsan's house is very beautiful."

1.5 More on the Nature of Possessor Raising

As seen from our foregoing discussion, although languages may vary with respect to the PR operation along with the options that are available, PR itself, as a syntactic process, can be formalized quite generally as in (14), which basically says "Move a possessor NP out of a Spec/NP position." Questions as to where it may move and what it may leave behind are constrained by general principles, such as the Case Filter and the θ-Criterion. In terms of formal properties, PR resembles typical types of NP-Movement, such as Subject Raising and Passivization among others, in some important respects. The landing site for PR-moved NPs, for example, has to be Case-marked and non-thematic just like that of the NPs moved by Subject Raising and Passivization. Given this consideration, Possessor Raising can be generalized alongside Subject Raising and Passivization under the general syntactic process of NP-Movement, and NP-Movement, in turn, is subsumed under an even more general rule: Move-α, i.e. Move anything anywhere. In other words, in the core formal grammar, there is no such rule as "Possessor Raising," although we will continue to use the term for convenience. The so-called "Possessor Raising" and "Passivization" now are just instantiations of one simple rule "Move-α" under the constraint of interacting principles. As noted above, the landing site of a raised possessor NP is jointly determined by the Case Filter and the θ-Criterion. In this section, we shall move on to illustrate that how far a possessor NP may move is also well constrained by the Subjacency condition, and why possessor NPs move at all.

1.5.1 Subjacency

It is noted that the Subjacency condition is observed in the Chinese Possessor Raising construction. Recall that three types of PR are instantiated in Chinese: A possessor NP may raise up into three distinctive syntactic positions: [1] the subject position of a passive or ergative construction (Section 1.2); [2] the Spec position of a complement VP (Section 1.3.2); and [3] an outer subject position (Section 1.3.3). Now consider the contrast between sentences under (a) and (b) below.

(98) a. <u>Zhangsan</u>$_i$ bei qiang-le t_i qianbao.
    Zhangsan BEI rob-ASP   wallet
    "Zhangsan was robbed of a wallet."

   b. *<u>Zhangsan</u>$_i$ bei qiang-le t_i taitai de qianbao.
    Zhangsan BEI rob-ASP wife DE wallet
    Intended meaning: "Zhangsan's wife was robbed of a wallet."

(99) a. <u>Lisi</u>$_i$ si-le t$_i$ henduo taoshu.

     Lisi die-ASP many peach-tree

     "Many of Lisi's peach trees died."

  b. *<u>Lisi</u>$_i$ si-le t$_i$ fuqin de henduo taoshu.

     Lisi die-ASP father DE many peach-tree

     Intended meaning: "Many of Lisi's father's peach trees died."

The contrast illustrated in the above two pairs of sentences could constitute a puzzle for a non-PR account of these sentences. On the reasonable assumption that the adversity effect generally applies to all of the above sentences, it is no less logical to say *Zhangsan* suffers from his wife's being robbed of a wallet than to say *Zhangsan* suffers from his own being robbed. Along a PR approach, this contrast can well be attributed to an effect of the Subjacency condition, which generally constrains all types of movement. As assumed in previous sections, CP, crucially not IP, and NP are bounding nodes for movement in Chinese. The movement of possessor NPs crosses two bounding nodes (i.e. two NPs circled) in sentences under (a) while it crosses only one bounding node (one NP) in sentences under (b), hence the grammatical contrast. (100) and (101) are illustrations of the derivation for the unacceptable sentences (98b) and (99b) respectively.

(100)

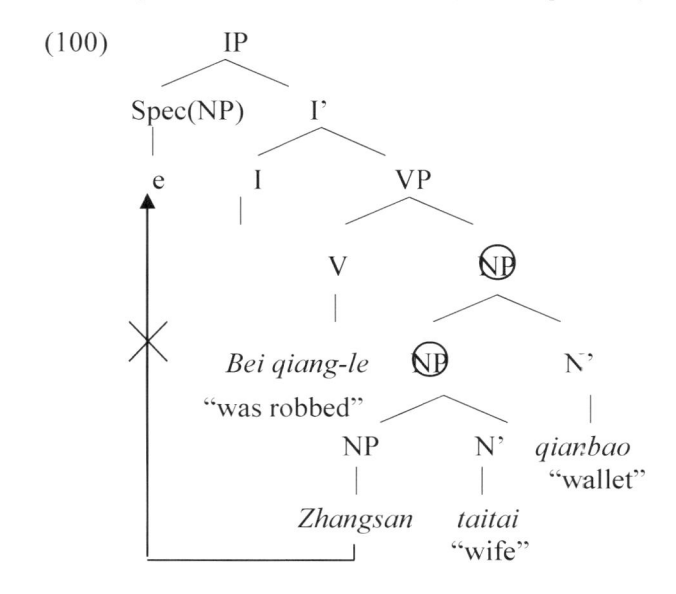

(101)

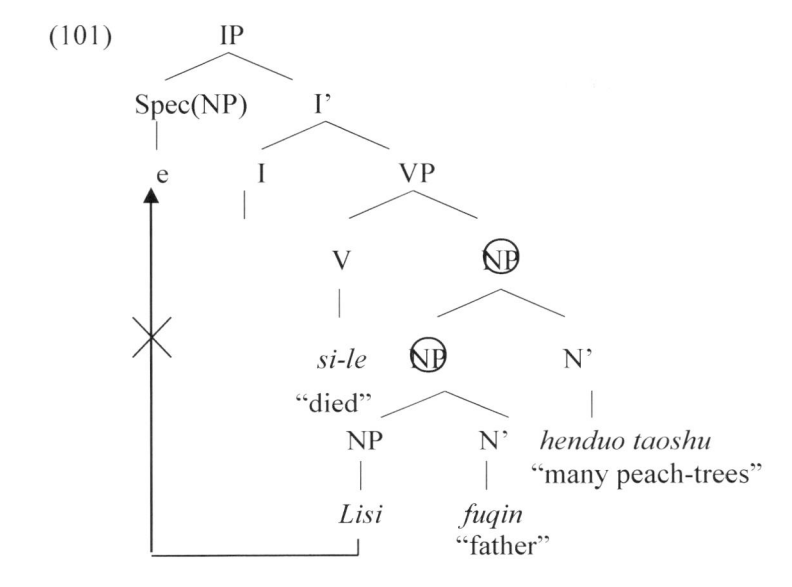

The Subjacency condition is also strictly observed in the application of PR that moves a possessor NP from the Spec position of an inner subject into that of an outer one in those double/multiple-subject constructions. In the following examples, (102) is well-formed since the movement crosses only one node, i.e. the containing NP, whereas (103) is ill-formed since it is forced through the containing NP plus a CP. (104) illustrates the derivation of (103).

(102) Zhangsan$_i$ t$_i$ fangzi hen piaoliang.
　　　Zhangsan　　house very beautiful
　　　"Zhangsan's house is very beautiful."

(103) *Zhangsan$_i$ Lisi xiangxin t$_i$ fangzi hen piaoliang.
　　　Zhangsan Lisi believe house very beautiful
　　　Intended meaning: "Lisi believes that Zhangsan's house is very beautiful."

(104)

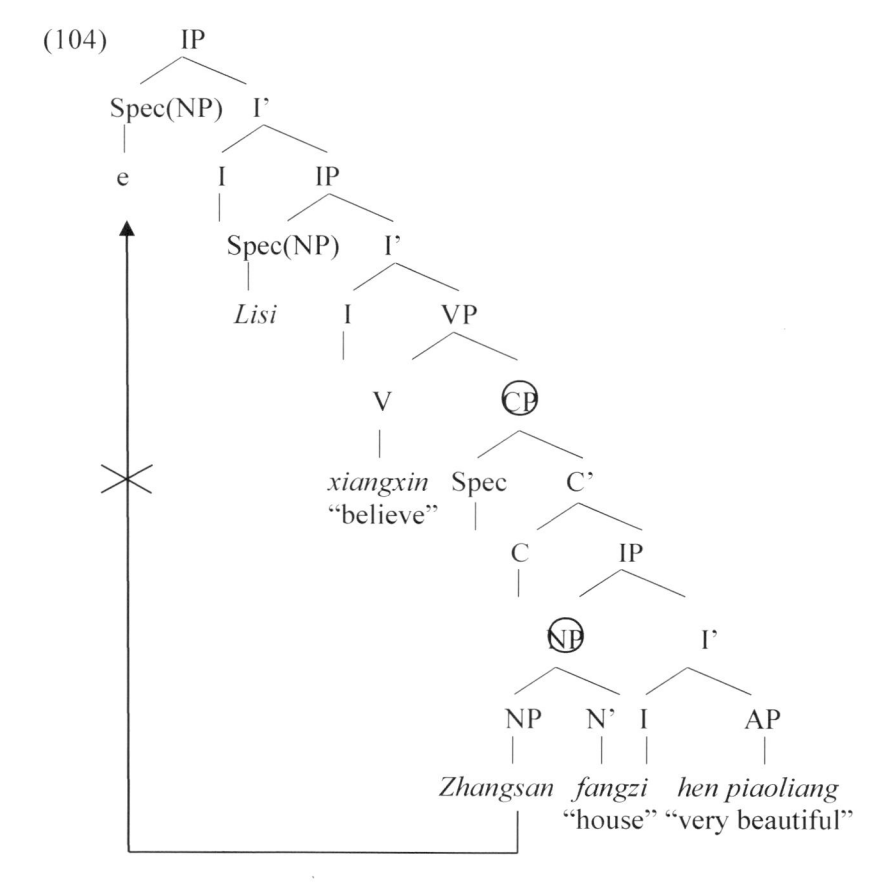

The Subjacency condition works exactly in the same way in the Korean and English Possessor Raising construction as in Chinese. Imagine a situation in which John's father accidentally left his camera in John's house and then on next evening a thief broke John's door and took away some valuable things including his father's camera. Although conceptually nothing is wrong with it, (105) is nevertheless ungrammatical.

(105) *John was robbed of (his/the) father's camera.

1.5.2 Motivating Possessor Raising

Given the flexibility of Move-α and the interaction of general principles, we argue that there is no such a rule as "Possessor Raising" in the core grammar. However, this claim does not mean that PR is not distinguishable from other types of movement such as "Passivization" and "Subject Raising." Although they are similar in terms of formal properties, they may still be distinguishable in functions and pragmatics. As Chomsky (1981) notes, although such a construction-particular rule as "Passivization" can be decomposed into more fundamental principles, there must be such a functional role as "suppressing of (semantic) subject" existing at some level of linguistic representation other than in the formal grammar. In this sense, Possessor Raising is distinguishable from other instances of movement. The functional role of PR can be specified as "separating the possessor from the whole NP, probably to emphasize the action's effect on the possessor, e.g. the adversity effect in languages like Chinese." After this functional role, as a sort of first motivation, has been instructed to the formal grammar, the latter will process it in its own way. Presumably, there is such a functional necessity in every language, but Possessor Raising as a syntactic process may work out in many different ways, depending on which and how options are selected from the menu of UG and on what the relevant lexical and morphological properties of particular languages are.

Moreover, a second important difference also exists between Possessor Raising on the one hand and Passivization /Subject Raising on the other: The latter, but not the former, is the only option that can save a sentence from potential violations of relevant principles. Passive sentences contain a passive morpheme picked up from the lexicon that absorbs the Case-assigning capacity of the main verb, so the D-Structure object NP, which is dependent on the passivized verb for Case-assignment, has to move through the process of Passivization and has no other choices. As a defining property, Subject Raising constructions always have an NP in a Caseless position, i.e. the subject position of an infinite embedded clause. And as required by the Case Filter, Subject Raising has to apply to move the NP to Case-marked position, i.e. the subject position of the finite matrix sentence.

But this is not the case for Possessor Raising. In the Possessor Raising construction, the possessor NP may always remain in its D-Structure Spec position without moving anywhere. And even when the containing NP as a whole unit moves, the possessor NP, still being in its Spec/NP DS position, just needs to follow as a case of Pied-Piping. In other words, in terms of formal properties, Possessor Raising can be ideally subsumed under NP-movement (or Move-α) along with Passivization and Subject Raising, but it is different from them in initial motivation. The latter two can largely be taken as resulting from syntactic motivations whereas the former functions just to achieve certain functional effect. In short, it can be concluded that Possessor Raising is optional syntactically, but obligatory functionally or pragmatically. This feature explains why Possessor Raising is not as commonly observed as Passivization and Subject Raising in natural languages.

1.6 Summary

Drawing on data from Chinese, Korean and English, this article has suggested that Possessor Raising (PR) is a syntactic process which is functional cross-linguistically. Being formalized as "Move a possessor NP out from a Spec/NP position," PR can be subsumed along with Passivization and Subject Raising under the general syntactic process "NP-Movement" in terms of formal syntactic properties, and all these processes are different types of instantiation of the UG rule — Move- α. It has also been argued that what distinguish PR from other types of NP-Movement are not formal syntactic features, but rather the motivations that initiate the movement in the first place. While the movement of both Passivization and Subject Raising is initiated by formal syntactic reasons, especially the Case Filter, PR movement is largely driven by functional purposes — separating the possessor NP from the possession NP to emphasize the former. Moreover, it has been demonstrated that the operation of PR is well under the constraint of UG principles in interaction with independently explainable language-particular properties. In particular, PR operation is mainly determined by the following three factors: [1] Whether the possessor NP can be properly

Case-marked in its new site; [2] Whether the nominal residue left behind by the PR movement can be Case-marked; and [3] Whether other relevant conditions on movement such as the Subjacency condition can be satisfied.

Most of the arguments in support of our proposal are constructed on the basis of the analysis of some language phenomena from Chinese, Korean, and English: the Chinese passive and ergative constructions with post-verbal "retained object"; the Chinese *BA*-construction with post-verbal "retained object"; the Korean double/multiple Nominative/Accusative construction; the Chinese double/multiple subject construction, the inalienable prepositional phrases such as *Mary punched John in the nose* in English, and the double object construction in all the above three languages. Our analysis in turn provides principled accounts for these superficially un-related phenomena. Our account is principled and therefore more explanatory because it is adequate not only to explain the phenomena observed in some languages, but also to explain why similar phenomena are not attested in others.

Several assumptions are crucial to reach our conclusions, and the latter, in turn, can be interpreted as having provided additional arguments for the former: [1] Larson's proposal about the VP structure, that is, a VP may recursively consist of an empty V taking another VP as its complement (Larson (1988)); [2] Xu's parametric theory of INFL, which states that the nature of INFL in languages like Chinese and Korean is fundamentally different from that of languages like English and French. As a result of a parameter-setting, the Chinese and Korean INFL has a phonetically null functional category [Predicator] only in its contents, whereas the English and French INFL contains the three elements [Tense, Agr, Predicator] in its contents (Xu (2003)).

In the course of our discussion, we also made a number of non-trivial claims related to the approach described in this article: [1] The inherent Partitive Case as a Case-assignment option may be available only in some languages such as Chinese and Finnish but not in others, such as English and Korean; [2] CP (but not IP) and NP are bounding nodes with respect to the Subjacency condition on movement in Chinese and Korean; and even more remarkably [3] the trace of an out-moved verb inherits Case-assigning capacity (i.e. the capacity to assign the structural Accusative Case) from the verb and then assigns it to a separate NP independently. In some languages, including Chinese and English, Case-assignment by the trace of a verb is subject to condition (30), whereas it is not in Korean. As demonstrated, this relatively simple assumption yields a set of desirable consequences including: (A) the one-to-one correspondence between Case assignors and assignees obtained, (B) Case-absorption by the passive morpheme can be specified more precisely as absorbing one and only one Case-assigning capacity of the verb that carries the morpheme without affecting any others, and (C) the Korean double/multiple Accusative constructions can be treated naturally in much the same way as the cross-linguistic double object construction.

Notes

[1] Details aside, under 'the Unaccusative Hypothesis' (Perlmutter (1978) and Burzio (1986)) verbs are divided into two classes: unaccusatives and unergatives. It is argued that the superficial subject of an unergative verb is also the D-Structure subject, it is base-generated there and remains there, whereas the superficial subject of an unaccusative verb, in fact, is the D-Structure object moving from an object position to a subject position through a derivation.

[2] Larson (1988) also tries to associate the verb's capacity of assigning structural Objective Case (=Accusative Case) to the fact that it is governed by the INFL head. The structural Objective Case, in his words, is essentially assigned by INFL through the governed V as its 'host'. In this article we are not going to accept this complication of assignment of structural Accusative Case, since conceptually there are no principled reasons to make this claim, and empirically this claim will leave the Korean multiple assignments of Accusative Case unaccounted for.

[3] In the sense that the two Accusative Cases are both structural, our proposal is similar to Jaeggli's (1986).

[4] Note also that the Adjacency condition on Case assignment does not hold in Korean as an instance of Long-distance Case-assignment. A full exploration of this issue is beyond the scope of this study.

[5] There are a number of proposals about the Korean multiple Accusative and multiple Nominative phenomena in the literature, most of which have been done in different theoretical frameworks such as Category Grammar and Relational Grammar, so they are largely not comparable to the one offered here. Rather

than taking readers through those proposals, we simply refer those interested to O'Grady (1991) for a good summary of the relevant issues.

[6] In associating Case-assigning properties of verbs to their thematic-role assigning properties, the proposal given in (30) is similar in spirit to Chomsky (1986) and Chomsky and Lasnik (1993), but advances in the opposite direction. Chomsky and Lasnik are trying to construe Case assignment as a condition on thematic-role assignment through the so-called 'Visibility condition.' But obviously the intuition behind the two proposals is the same. We will not get into details on this issue here.

[7] Condition (30) basically says that only if a verb may assign separate thematic roles to the NPs, then the verb and its trace may assign the Accusative Case to separate NPs. This condition holds true in various languages. However, as an anonymous referee correctly points out, this condition does not seem to be observed in Korean, so in that language, a verb and its trace may assign Accusative Case to two separate NPs regardless of whether the verb assigns two separate thematic roles to the NPs. In other words, condition (30) may be language-particular and sometimes can be relaxed. Although this is a largely open question for future work, we would like to note that the condition may even be relaxed in Chinese and English under certain circumstances. For instance, although *dasui* 'break' in Chinese and *cook* in English are both regular and typical transitive verbs, they may take up two separate NPs as their objects under certain syntactic environments, as seen in the following two sentences. See Xu (2004) for further discussion on the issue.

(i)   Zhangsan dasui-le ta san.ge beizi.

Zhangsan break-ASP him three cups

"Zhangsan broke him three cups.'

(ii) Mary cooked John a meal.

[8] Sentence (33) is taken from Li (1985). An anonymous referee has kindly pointed out that (33) may not be a grammatical sentence. We carried out a language survey after this was pointed out and found that its grammaticality is marginal indeed, since some native speakers accept it, while others find it not perfectly natural. We keep this sentence here but put a question mark (?) before it.

[9] A similar situation is also observed in the Chinese *BEI*-construction. Although Chinese, like English, has passive constructions (i.e. the *BEI*-construction), many English passive sentences cannot be naturally translated into the Chinese *BEI*-construction. You may find the Chinese passive equivalent to *John was cheated on*

by Mary in English, for example, but not a passive equivalent to *John was loved by Mary*. However, it should be noted that this contrast has nothing to do with formal syntax. Rather, it is a matter of purely lexical property of *BEI* (i.e. the 'adversity' property) that must be specified in the lexicon.

[10] The same single parameter-setting may give rise to many cross-linguistic contrasts: whether Null Subjects are allowed; whether AP/NP alone can function as predicates; and whether reflexives are permitted in the subject positions of finite clauses, just to name a few. See Xu (2003) for details.

[11] According to Xu (2003), although their verbs are Tense-inflected, Korean and Japanese, like Chinese, fix the INFL parameter in the Chinese way, since the two languages lack a crucial element [Agr].

[12] O'Grady (1991) offers a very interesting discussion of the Case alternation phenomenon in Korean. Although it is difficult to compare different accounts formulated in different theoretical frameworks, what makes us skeptical about his proposal is that it is not cross-linguistically falsifiable since it just explains why Korean allows Case-marking alternations and multiple Case assignments but not why, say, English does not.

[13] I thank Sungki Suh for helping me with the Korean data cited here.

Chapter **2**

Two Types of Pre-Verbal Reflexives in Chinese[*]

ABSTRACT: *In this chapter, it is demonstrated that the Chinese reflexive ziji "self" in a pre-verbal position can be either an adverbial or a subject. Adverbial and subject reflexive are subject to different types of locality conditions. Adverbial reflexives are local because adverbials in general are local, while the fact that subject reflexives, as anaphors, are local is an effect of the relevant Binding condition. Subject and adverbial reflexives are not distinguished from each other in Chinese as obviously as they are in English. An adverb diagnostic tool has been developed to differentiate the real subject reflexives from adverbial ones.*

2.1 Long-Distance and Local Anaphors in Chinese

It has been widely observed that there is a sharp contrast between the Chinese bare reflexive *ziji* and compound reflexives (i.e. pronoun + *ziji*, such as *taziji* "himself/herself" and *womenziji* "ourselves") in that the former, but not the latter, may permit long-distance antecedents, especially when those reflexives occur in the post-verbal (object) position. The following pair of sentences illustrates this contrast (see Huang and Tang (1988) and Cole, Hermon, and Sung (1990) among many others).

---

[*]A version of this chapter originally appeared with the title "Two Types of Pre-Verbal Anaphors in Chinese" in *Journal of Chinese Language and Computing* 18:1 (2008), pp. 25–32. Revisions made are technical and minimal, the essential contents remain unchanged. It is included in this monograph as a chapter with kind permission from the Chinese and Oriental Languages Information Processing Society, Singapore.

(1) Zhangsan$_i$ renwei Lisi$_j$ zeguai-le ziji$_{i/j}$.
    Zhangsan think Lisi blame-Asp self
    "Zhangsan thinks that Lisi blamed himself."

(2) Zhangsan$_i$ renwei Lisi$_j$ zeguai-le ta-ziji$_{*i/j}$.
    Zhangsan think   Lisi blame-Asp him-self
    "Zhangsan thinks that Lisi blamed himself."

Generally speaking, this is a correct observation. However, we notice that the situation may be obscure, and therefore much more complex when we take into consideration the phenomena exhibited in the following sentences where the reflexives occur pre-verbally.

(3) Zhangsan$_i$ yiwei Lisi$_j$ zhidao ziji$_{i/j}$ neng zuo na jian shi.
     Zhangsan thought Lisi know self able do that CL job
     "*Zhangsan thought that Lisi knew that himself was able to do that job."

(4) Zhangsan$_i$ yiwei Lisi$_j$ yinggai ziji$_{*i/j}$ neng zuo na jian shi.
     Zhangsan thought Lisi should self able do that CL job
     "Zhangsan thought that Lisi should be able to do that job himself."

(5) Zhangsan$_i$ xiangxin Lisi$_j$ zhidao ziji $_{i/j}$ xihuan kaiche.
     Zhangsan believe Lisi know self like driving
     "*Zhangsan believes that Lisi knows that himself likes driving."

(6) Zhangsan$_i$ xiangxin Lisi$_j$ jingchang ziji$_{*i/j}$ kaiche shangxue.
     Zhangsan believe Lisi often self driving go to school
     "Zhangsan believes that Lisi often goes to school by driving himself."

The existence of these sentences seems to suggest that there is something else at work, in addition to the observed contrast between compound and bare reflexives that applies only to the pre-verbal reflexives and not to the post-verbal ones.

2.2 Local Anaphors in Chinese

We note first that the reflexives in some sentences above, particularly those which don't allow long-distance binding as in (4) and (6), are not the (argument) subject. Rather, it is functionally an (adjunct) adverbial. If this is so, there are, in fact, two types of reflexives, subject and adverbial reflexives, which both occur pre-verbally in languages like Chinese. It is worth noting here that adverbial reflexives are not peculiar to Chinese. In English, for example, reflexives may also take a non-argument position, which is very similar to the Chinese phenomenon that we are now considering. The reflexive *himself* in the following English sentences, as noted in Bickerton (1987),[1] is clearly not an argument. The semantics of this type of reflexive, which can be roughly characterized as "NP_i, and no one but NP_i," is also different from the semantics of argument reflexives.

(7) a. John himself did it.

   b. John did it himself.

(8) a. John gave it to Mary himself.

   b. John himself gave it to Mary.

Being different in syntactic nature from each other, subject and adverbial reflexives are expected to behave differently, and therefore should be treated differently in both Chinese and English. Note that it is not difficult to tell whether a reflexive in a given context is used as a subject or as an adverbial in English, since the language has inflectional morphology and adverbials (but not subjects) can be placed either before or after the verb. In Chinese, on the other hand, one may easily be confused as to whether a certain reflexive is the subject or an adverbial in a clause, as these two types of constituents both occur pre-verbally in the language, and the language allows null subjects and has little morphology. Such a distinction obviously has to be drawn before any appropriate characterization of the properties of subject reflexives can be achieved.

2.3 Distinction between Two Types of Reflexives

To distinguish between these two types of pre-verbal reflexives in Chinese, we note that although the relative linear ordering of adverbs and adverbial expressions is generally quite free in the language, Chinese has a class of adverbs whose position is relatively fixed. They can occur only after the subject NP but not before it, and these adverbs must precede all other adverbs and adverbial expressions used in the sentence. *Yinggai* "should" and *jingchang* "often", among many others, are two such adverbs. Thus, sentences "<u>a</u>" in (9)–(12) below, which satisfy this constraint, are acceptable, while sentences <u>b</u>, which are in violation of it, are not.

(9)   a. Ni yinggai mai yi dong fangzi.
          you should buy one CL house
          "You should buy a house."

      b. *Yinggai ni mai yi dong fangzi.
          should you buy one CL house

(10) a. Zhangsan jingchang kaiche shangxue.
          Zhangsan often drive go to school
          "Zhangsan often goes to school by driving."

      b. *Jingchang Zhangsan kaiche shangxue.
          often Zhangsan drive go to school

(11) a. Wo yinggai manmande du.
          I should slowly read
          "I should read slowly."

      b. *Wo manmande yinggai du.
          I slowly should read

(12) a. Zhangsan jingchang zai jia xie wenzhang.
          Zhangsan often at home write paper
          "Zhangsan often writes papers at home."

      b. *Zhangsan zai jia jingchang xie wenzhang
          Zhangsan at home often write paper

Note that this constraint on word-ordering, regardless of how the constraint itself can be explained, could be used as a diagnostic tool to distinguish subject and adverbial reflexives for our purpose. If an reflexive occurs before such adverbs as in (13) and (14) below, the reflexive must be a subject of the clause since adverbs of that kind can never follow a subject NP. Following the same line of reasoning, if an reflexive is placed after such adverbs as in (15) and (16), it should best be treated as an adverbial.

(13) Zhangsan $_i$ renwei ziji $_i$ yinggai qu nali.
 Zhangsan think self should go there
 "*Zhangsan thinks that himself should go over there."

(14) Zhangsan $_i$ shuo ziji $_i$ jingchang kaiche.
 Zhangsan say self often drive
 "*Zhangsan says that himself often drives."

(15) Zhangsan$_i$ renwei Lisi$_j$ yinggai ziji$_{*i/j}$ qu nali.
 Zhangsan think Lisi should self go there
 "Zhangsan thinks Lisi should go over there himself."

(16) Zhangsan$_i$ shuo EC$_j$ jingchang ziji$_{*i/j}$ kaiche.
 Zhangsan say often self drive
 "Zhangsan says that (he) often drives by himself."

As in the previous examples, the adverbial *ziji* in (15) and (26) is strictly local in nature. It can co-refer only with the closest subject (i.e. *Lisi* in (15) and an empty pronoun in (16)) but not with the subject of the matrix clause (i.e. *Zhangsan* in both (15) and (16)). In contrast, the subject *ziji* (17) and (18) below can be long-distance. It may co-refer either with the closest subject *Zhangsan* or with the matrix subject *Lisi*, bypassing the closest subject.

(17) Lisi$_i$ shuo Zhangsan$_j$ renwei ziji$_{i/j}$ yinggai qu nali.
 Lisi say Zhangsan think self should go there
 "*Lisi says that Zhangsan thinks that himself should go over there."

(18) Lisi$_i$ bu xiangxin Zhangsan$_j$ shuo ziji$_{i/j}$ jingchang kaiche.
      Lisi not believe Zhangsan say self often drive
      "*Lisi does not believe that Zhangsan says that himself often
      drives."

Note that if we assume that the long-distance property of the Chinese
reflexive in the real subject position can be derived along some form of
LF-movement approach, such as those suggested in Huang et al. (1988)
and Cole et al. (1990),[2] the natural question that arises here is why the
same reflexive (at least morphologically) behaves differently in different
syntactic positions.

2.4 The Syntactic Nature of Local Reflexives in Chinese

We would point out that the local nature of adverbial reflexives is
fundamentally different from that of non-adverbial reflexives. Conceptually,
while non-adverbial reflexives as argument NPs with no inherent reference
seek antecedents for their reference, and in this sense they are called
"anaphoric," the adverbial reflexives essentially "emphasize" the subject
NPs, namely "NP$_i$, and no one but NP$_i$" in the words of Bickerton (1987).
Thus adverbial reflexives are "emphatic." Anaphoric reflexives are local in
the sense of Binding Theory in that they require the antecedents, on which
their reference is dependent, to be close to them, while emphatic reflexives
are local in the sense that they emphasize only the closest subject NPs.
Clearly, the nature of locality of reflexives in the adverbial sense is not
a peculiar property of adverbial reflexives, but rather that of adverbs and
adverbial expressions in general.[3]

In addition to the contrast between the adverbial *ziji* and the non-
adverbial *ziji* discussed above, the following contrasts, which may otherwise
be puzzling, also become more understandable in light of our general
observation that a reflexive in Chinese may be an argument anaphor or an
adverbial one, and that adverbial reflexives are "local" because adverbials
in general are local.

(A) The contrast between the Chinese reciprocal *huxiang* and the non-
adverbial *ziji*

We observe that the Chinese reciprocal *huxiang*, unlike the bare reflexive *ziji* in non-adverbial usage, is also "local," as is the adverbial reflexive *ziji*.

(19) [Zhangsan he Lisi]$_i$ zhidao tamen$_j$ huxiang$*_{i/j}$ aimu.
Zhangsan and Lisi know they each other love
"Zhangsan and Lisi know that they love each other."

(20) Laoshi-men$_i$ shuo zhexie xuesheng$_j$ jingchang huxiang$*_{i/j}$
teacher-pl say these students often each other
bangzhu.
help
"The teachers say that these students help each other very often."

We attribute the locality of the Chinese reciprocal to its placement in the adverbial position in the same way we did with the adverbial *ziji*. That is, the Chinese reciprocal is local because adverbials are all local.

(B) The contrast between the Chinese reciprocal *huxiang* and the English reciprocal *each other*

While the Chinese reciprocal *huxiang* can only be interpreted as strictly local, as illustrated in (19) and (20), the English reciprocal *each other*, as Lebeaux (1983) demonstrates, has some interesting properties when compared to its Chinese counterpart. Consider sentence (21) (= Lebeaux 20) below. It has two interpretations: one in which *John* and *Mary* both know the full content of the embedded proposition and a second in which each knows only his or her own feelings and not the other's. We would like to interpret the sentence with the long-distance reading (or narrow scope reading in Lebeaux's terms), as having a long-distance anaphor, *each other*.

(21) [John and Mary]$_i$ knew that they$_i$ liked each other$_i$.

a. John and Mary knew that [John liked Mary/Mary liked John]

b. John knew that John liked Mary
Mary knew that Mary liked John
[Interpretation: John and Mary each knew that each liked the other.]

If this observation is correct, no matter what kind of explanation we can provide for it,[4] there will be a clear contrast between the English *each other* and the Chinese reciprocal *huxiang*, since the Chinese equivalent of (21) can only have one of the two possible interpretations, namely the one which corresponds to (21a). For us, this contrast between Chinese and English reciprocals is no surprise. The Chinese reciprocal *huxiang* can only be interpreted locally because it occurs in the pre-verbal adverbial position (recall that the object NP always follows the verb in the language), and *each other* can be long-distantly interpreted because it occurs in a post-verbal argument position.

2.5 Summary

It has been widely observed that there is a sharp contrast between the Chinese bare reflexive *ziji* and compound reflexives (i.e. pronoun + *ziji*, such as *taziji* "himself/herself" and *womenziji* "ourselves") in that the former, but not the latter, may permit long-distance antecedents, especially when those reflexives occur in the post-verbal (object) position. Although this is a correct observation, it has to be pointed out that the reflexive in some types of sentences don't allow long-distance binding. It has been argued in this chapter that those reflexives that don't permit long-distance interpretation are not the (argument) subject in the first place, which is comparable to the English reflexive *himself* in such a sentence as *John gave it to Mary himself.* Rather, it is functionally an (adjunct) adverbial. If so, there are, in fact, two types of reflexives, subject and adverbial reflexives, which both occur pre-verbally in languages like Chinese. Adverbial and subject reflexives are subject to different types of locality conditions. In addition, the locality nature of adverbial reflexives is fundamentally different from that of non-adverbial reflexives. Adverbial reflexives are local because adverbials, in general, are local, while the fact that the subject reflexives are local is an effect of the relevant Binding condition on anaphors. The Chinese language allows subject reflexives in the position where English excludes reflexives because the INFL in Chinese does not contain the element Agr (Xu (2003), among others). An adverb diagnostic has been developed to differentiate the real subject reflexives from adverbial ones.

Furthermore, some other contrasts that may otherwise be puzzling also become more understandable based on this general observation that a reflexive in Chinese may be an argument anaphor or an adverbial, and that adverbial reflexives are "local" because adverbials in general are local: (A) The contrast between the Chinese reciprocal *huxiang* and the non-adverbial reflexive *ziji*; *and* (B) The contrast between the Chinese reciprocal *huxiang* and the English reciprocal *each other.*

Notes

[1] *He himself* was treated as a single constituent in Bickerton (1987). But since they are separable, each occupying a position, we would treat them separately. *Himself* is an adverbial reflexive, while *he* is an argument.

[2] Note that the LF-movement approach of Huang et al. (1988) and Cole et al. (1990) fails to account for the contrast exhibited here

[3] Take a simple English sentence like *John says that Bill always goes to school early*. Note that the adverb *always* can be associated with the local subject *Bill* but not the 'long-distance' subject *John*, a kind of locality.

[4] If one adopts the general approach of Lebeaux (1983), the account will be related to the possibility of LF-movement.

Chapter **3**

The Positioning of Chinese Focus Marker *SHI* and Pied-Piping in Logical Form[*]

ABSTRACT: *Two groups of Chinese sentences involve LF wh-movement in the same fashion, but contrast sharply in grammaticality. We demonstrate in this chapter that this systematic contrast constitutes a significant problem for the well-known claim that the LF movement of adjuncts is constrained by the applicable locality conditions, whereas that of arguments need not obey those conditions in the wh-in-situ languages like Chinese. We argue that this contrast can be accounted for naturally by appealing to a general condition on the positioning of the Chinese focus marker shi, which has nothing to do with the locality conditions on movement in any form. Furthermore, a reasonable solution of the problem argues for a Pied-Piping approach to deal with the language facts that have been considered by many authors, but have not received a satisfactory treatment. That is, what is being LF-extracted in those superficially island-violating sentences, in fact, is the whole island that contains the questioned or focused element, rather than the questioned or focused element alone. The LF movement of arguments is subject to the very same locality conditions as that of adjuncts in the Chinese language.*

[*]A version of this chapter originally appeared with the same title in *Journal of Chinese Linguistics* 38:1 (2010), pp. 134–156. Revisions are technical and minimal, the essential contents remain the same. It is included in this monograph as a chapter with kind permission from the *Journal of Chinese Linguistics*, Hong Kong.

3.1 Posing the Problem

Since the important works of Huang (1982a/b), among others, it has been widely assumed that although the formation of questions and cleft sentences does not involve any movement in Syntax, it is reasonable to postulate that they undergo movement in the Logical Form (LF) component of grammar in languages like Chinese, Korean and Japanese.[1] Thus, for example, while it is clear that sentences like (1)–(3) below are generated in the Syntax with the *wh*-phrase, the focused phrase and the focused *wh*-phrase never move anywhere but in their base positions. It has been argued that in the LF interpretive component, each of those phrases is moved as a (quasi-) quantifier to an operator position c-commanding the sentence, leaving a trace interpreted as a variable bound to it (FM = Focus marker *shi*).

(1) Ni xihuan shei?
    you like who
    "Who do you like?"
    LF: [shei$_i$ [ni xihuan t$_i$]]
        who you like

(2) Shi wo mingtian yao mai neiben shu.
    FM I tomorrow want buy that book
    "It is I who want to buy that book tomorrow."
    LF: [(shi wo)$_i$ [t$_i$ mingtian yao mai neiben shu]]
        FM I   tomorrow want buy that book

(3) Shi shei da-le ta?
    FM who beat-Asp him
    "Who is it that has beat him?"
    LF: [(shi shei)$_i$ [t$_i$ da-le ta]]
        FM who   beat-Asp him

With regard to the effects of the locality conditions such as Complex Noun Phrase Constraint (CNPC) in the LF-Movement of this sort, Huang (1982a) argues that there is an important contrast between arguments and adjuncts.[2] While the LF-movement of adjuncts, very much like the syntactic movement of their English counterparts, is well constrained by the applicable locality conditions (as in (4) below), the LF-movement of arguments need not obey those conditions ((5) and (6)). Due to the nature of the Chinese Focus marker *shi* (lit. "to be") as an adverbial in this usage,[3] the LF-movement of the focused constituents, regardless of whether they are *wh*-phrases or not, and regardless of whether they are arguments or adjuncts, obeys the locality conditions ((7) and (8)).

(4) *[[$_{NP}$ Ni weisheime mai de gou] zui gui]?
　　　　　you why 　　 buy DE dog most expensive
　　Compare: "*Dogs that you bought why are most expensive?"

(5) [[$_{NP}$ Shei mai de gou] zui gui]?
　　　　who buy DE dog most expensive
　　Compare: "*Dogs that who bought are most expensive?"

(6) [ni xihuan [$_{NP}$ wo piping shei de wenzhang]]?
　　you like 　　 I criticize who DE article
　　Compare: "*You like articles in which I criticize who?"

(7) *[wo xihuan [$_{NP}$ shi Zhangsan mai de gou]]].
　　 I like 　　 FM Zhangsan buy DE dog
　　Compare: "*I like the dog that it is Zhangsan that bought."

(8) *[ni xihuan [$_{NP}$ shi shei mai de gou]]?
　　you like 　　 FM who buy DE dog
　　Compare: "*Do you like the dog that who is it that bought?"

Huang's account for language facts of this sort is crucially based on the classical disjunctive version of the Empty Category Principle (ECP) (Chomsky (1981), and Lasnik and Saito (1984), among others), which basically states that a non-pronominal empty category (= a trace) must either be lexically governed or locally controlled, i.e. governed by its antecedents. Thus, the *wh*-phrase *shei* "who" in (6), being lexically governed by the verb *piping* "criticize", may move freely in LF, crossing two or more bounding nodes because its trace will be in no violation of the ECP, and the LF-movement of this sort is simply not subject to the Subjacency condition in the first place. Sentence (5) is well-formed because the island-embedded trace of the LF-moved phrase is also lexically governed by the INFL, although not by the verb. INFL, on another crucial assumption of Huang, is "lexical" in Chinese.[4] In contrast, a question like (4) with an adjunct *wh-*phrase *weisheime* "why", if LF-moved out of a complex NP, is ill-formed, since the trace of the moved phrase is in violation of ECP as it can neither be lexically governed nor locally controlled.[5] Since the Focus marker *shi* is a non-objectual adverbial, whatever follows it will pattern with non-objectual, adjunct operators rather than with objectual argument ones, thus sentences like (7) and (8) above are both ungrammatical as Huang's (1982a) proposal predicts.

Seen in the light of some important works, we note that Huang's general proposal and his arguments are questionable. First of all, as noted above, Huang's account of the extraction possibilities of the subject NP is crucially based on his Lexical INFL Hypothesis. This hypothesis is problematic. Functional categories like INFL are functional universally. The language facts captured under the Lexical INFL Hypothesis can be better recast and reinterpreted in principled ways (Xu (2003)). Second, with regards to the Chinese Focus Construction, it is entirely speculative to postulate that a constituent with Focus marker *shi*, regardless of whether it was an argument or an adjunct originally, functions like an adjunct with respect to LF-movement. It is generally agreed that relationships such as that between a verb and an argument or adjunct are fundamentally determined, and thus cannot change during the course of a derivation. Third, the disjunctive version of ECP that Huang's approach crucially depends on is in question also, especially if we adopt an approach developed in Aoun, Hornstein, Lightfoot, and Weinberg (1987) by which the ECP is split: lexical/head government is a requirement for all empty categories that are visible at the level of Phonetic Form (PF),[6] not merely one of two options, while and antecedent government, subsumed under the Theory of Generalized Binding, is necessary for all anaphors, regardless of whether they are empty or lexical at the LF level as long as it has a Domain. The PF requirement of head government, now, is simply irrelevant for this type of Chinese sentences, as the residue of LF-movement in the language is invisible at the PF level of representation.

Finally, in addition to these conceptual problems, Huang's proposal cannot explain some important empirical facts, such as the sentences listed below. These facts, which are systematically observed in Chinese, bear directly on the issues under consideration, but have been neglected in many works on the issues.

(9) Shi <u>Zhangsan</u> mai de gou zui ke-ai.
      FM Zhangsan buy DE dog cutest
      Compare: "*The dog that it is Zhangsan that bought is the cutest.'

(9') The LF-representation according to Huang's proposal:
      [(shi Zhangsan)$_i$ [$_{NP}$ [$_{CP}$ t$_i$ mai de] gou] zui ke-ai]]
       FM Zhangsan   buy DE dog cutest

(10) Shi <u>shei</u> mai de gou zui ke-ai?
      FM who buy DE dog cutest
      Compare: "*The dog that who is it that bought is the cutest?"

(10') The LF-representation according to Huang's proposal:
      [(shi shei)$_i$ [$_{NP}$ [$_{CP}$ t$_i$ mai de] gou] zui ke-ai]]
       FM who   buy DE dog cutest

(11) Wo xiang-zhidao shi <u>shei</u> mai de gou zui ke-ai.
      I   wonder   FM who buy DE dog cutest
      Compare: "*I wonder the dog that who is it that bought is the cutest."

(11') The LF-representation according to Huang's proposal:
      Wo xiang-zhidao [(shi shei)$_i$ [$_{NP}$ [$_{CP}$ t$_i$ mai de] gou] zui ke-ai]]
      I   wonder   FM who   buy DE dog cutest

Note that if Huang is correct, then the focused constituents underlined in each of the sentences, regardless of whether it is a *wh*-phrase or not, should be moved in LF, and the movement rule, as illustrated by the corresponding LF-representations (9'), (10'), and (11'), would have crossed the two bounding nodes NP and CP/S and would be in violation of the Subjacency condition.[7] Furthermore, the traces left by the movement would be in violation of ECP since the constituents with the Focus marker in front of them, under Huang's proposal, cannot be lexically governed. Nevertheless, these sentences are perfectly acceptable. Also, note that these acceptable sentences differ minimally from the unacceptable sentences cited in Huang's well known works in that the complex NPs occur in the subject position in sentences (9), (10), and (11), while the complex NPs occupy the object position in Huang's unacceptable sentences. To illustrate this point, we can even make up some new sentences whereby the very same complex NPs are placed in the object position. As seen in (12)–(14) below. The resultant sentences will then become unacceptable.

(12) *wo xihuan shi <u>Zhangsan</u> mai de gou.
     I   like   FM Zhangsan buy DE dog
    "*I like the dog that it is Zhangsan that bought."

(13) *Ni xihuan shi <u>shei</u> mai de gou?
    you like FM who buy DE dog
    "*You like the dog that who it is that bought?"

(14) *Wo xiang-zhidao ni xihuan shi <u>shei</u> mai de gou.
    I   wonder   you like FM who buy DE dog
    "*I wonder you like the dog that who is it that bought."

The contrast in grammaticality between (9)–(11) and (12)–(14), for Huang's proposal, is puzzling and thus demands an explanation. What is relevant is the nature of the to-be-moved quantificational expression and its relationship with the main verb within the complex NP, rather than the grammatical function of the complex NP itself. Note also that what Huang leaves unexplained is the grammaticality of (9)–(11), but not the ungrammaticality of (12)–(14). Given the structural similarities between the two types of sentences, the explanation cannot come from the Subjacency condition or from the ECP since, if any one of the two kinds of constraints is violated in one type of sentence, the same constraint would also be violated in another type in exactly the same fashion.

In this chapter, we are not going to concern ourselves with the above conceptual problems with Huang's proposal. Rather, we will focus our attention on the puzzling contrast exhibited between (9)–(11) and (12)–(14), attempting to work out an account for the contrast. It will be argued that a reasonable account for the language facts has nothing to do with either the Subjacency condition, the ECP, or any other forms of locality conditions, but it is crucially based on an analysis of the Chinese Focus Construction. Furthermore, it will be demonstrated that our new account for the facts, in turn, suggests quite clearly that some important language facts from Chinese have long been mishandled in the literature. A re-interpretation of the facts will lead us to a fresh way of looking at issues that have been under consideration by many authors for many years. Since our new proposal will be based on an analysis of the Chinese Focus Construction, we shall begin with a somewhat detailed discussion of the construction and its formal properties.

3.2 Some Formal Properties of the Chinese Focus Construction

The formation of a focus construction or a cleft sentence in Chinese clearly does not involve the dislocation of any constituent in Syntax. A focus construction differs from a non-focus one only in that in a focus construction there is a focus marker (the copula *shi*) immediately preceding the focused constituent.

(15) Shi <u>wo</u> mingtian cong Feicheng qu Niuyue.
       FM I tomorrow from Philadelphia go New York
       "It is I who will go to New York from Philadelphia tomorrow."

(16) Wo shi <u>mingtian</u> cong Feicheng qu Niuyue.
        I FM tomorrow from Philadelphia go New York
       "It is tomorrow when I will go to New York from Philadelphia."

(17) Wo mingtian shi <u>cong Feicheng</u> qu Niuyue.

     I tomorrow FM from Philadelphia go New York

     "It is from Philadelphia that I will go to New York

     tomorrow."

The Focus Marker *shi*, as argued in Teng (1979) and Xu and Li (1993), is not present at D-Structure (DS). It is reasonable to postulate that the marker is inserted later as an instance of Adjoin-α in the sense of Lebeaux (1991).[8] Adjoin-α, along with Move-α and Project-α, takes place in the course of the derivation of S-Structure (SS) from D-Structure (DS). The Focus marker insertion is triggered by an [F]-marking (i.e. the feature [+Focus]), which is assigned and/or checked at D-structure. This is to say that sentences (15)–(17) above have the form as in (15')–(17') respectively as their DS-representations, where they differ minimally in the assignment of [+F]-marking on different constituents.

(15') [wo] $^{[+F]}$ mingtian cong Feicheng qu Niuyue.

      I   tomorrow from Philadelphia go New York

(16') Wo [mingtian] $^{[+F]}$ cong Feicheng qu Niuyue.

(17') Wo mingtian [cong Feicheng] $^{[+F]}$ qu Niuyue.

According to Lebeaux's Principle of Licensing Well-Formedness, an element cannot be present until the relevant licensing relation allowing or requiring it in the phrase marker has applied. Note that neither the Projection Principle nor anything else requires the presence of FM *shi* at DS, otherwise the obvious similarities among sentences (15)–(17) above will not be properly captured. Thus, it is generally assumed that these sentences share the common DS representation in terms of basic structure, but have different assignments of the functional feature [+Focus], and the latter eventually triggers the insertion of the overt marker *shi* in front of different constituents.

Since a constituent of an embedded clause, just like that of a matrix sentence, can be a focused one, FM *shi* can also be inserted in front of it.

(18) Wo renwei shi <u>Zhangsan</u> xihuan Lisi.
    I think   FM Zhangsan like Lisi
    "I think that it is Zhangsan that likes Lisi."

In *wh*-questions, only the *wh*-phrases, but not any others, can be the focused constituents. We follow Xu and Li (1993) in assuming that this is because *wh* phrases are all marked [+Focus] in the lexicon and they carry the marking into the syntax when they themselves are composed into the phrase marker. As illustrated below, such a lexical marking interacts with the syntactic marking of focus in an interesting way.

(19) [Shei] $^{[+F]}$ mai-le neiben zidian?
    who   buy-Asp that dictionary
    "Who bought that dictionary?"

(20) Ni [shenme shihou] $^{[+F]}$ nian-de daxue?
    you what time   attend-Asp college
    "When did you attend college?"

If it is necessary, the overt Focus Marker *shi* may also be inserted to intensify the nature of the *wh*-phrase being a focused constituent, yielding sentences like following.

(19') Shi [shei] $^{[+F]}$ mai-le neiben zidian?
    FM who buy-Asp that dictionary
    "WHO bought that dictionary?"

(20') Ni shi [shenme shihou] $^{[+F]}$ nian-de daxue?
    you FM what time   attend-Asp college
    "WHEN did you attend college?"

Since the *wh*-phrase in a *wh*-question is automatically assigned the feature [+Focus], if *shi*, as an overt marker for foci, is to be inserted, it has to be inserted in a position immediately preceding the *wh* phrase obligatorily as shown in (21) and (22), otherwise an ungrammatical sentence would be generated (i.e. (23) and (24)).

(21) Shi <u>shei</u> mingtian qu Beijing?
FM who tomorrow go Beijing
"Who is it that will go to Beijing tomorrow?"

(22) Zhangsan shi <u>shenme-shihou</u> qu Beijing?
Zhangsan FM what-time go Beijing
"WHEN will Zhangsan go to Beijing?"

(23) *<u>Shei</u> shi mingtian qu Beijing?
who FM tomorrow go Beijing

(24) *Shi Zhangsan <u>shenme-shihou</u> qu Beijing?
FM Zhangsan what time   go Beijing

Interestingly, the insertion of the Focus Marker is not absolutely free. It is subject to some formal constraints. The Focus Marker, for example, can't be inserted into a position between a verb or a preposition and its object. Violating this constraint, the following sentences are unacceptable.

(25) *Ta zai xuexiao pengjian-le shi <u>Zhangsan</u>.
he on campus meet-Asp FM Zhangsan
Intended: "It is Zhangsan that he met on the campus."

(26) *Ta bei shi <u>Zhangsan</u> pian-le.
he by FM Zhangsan cheat-Asp
Intended: "It was Zhangsan that he was cheated by."

(27) *Ta zai xuexiao pengjian-le shi <u>shei</u>?
he on campus meet-Asp FM who
Intended: "Who was it that he met on the campus?"

(28) *Ta bei shi <u>shei</u> pian-le?
he by FM who cheat-Asp
Intended: "Who was it that he was cheated by?"

This constraint on the insertion of a Focus Marker can be reasonably attributed to the adjacency condition on the assignment of Accusative Case by a verb or a preposition, which prohibits any lexical constituent from intervening between Case assigners and assignees. This condition holds quite generally in Chinese and in many other languages. That the following sentences are unacceptable is simply due to the fact that an adverb intervenes between a verb or a preposition and its NP object.

(29) a. Ta <u>naixin-de</u> deng   wo.
           he patiently wait-for me
           "He was waiting for me patiently."

      b. *Ta deng <u>naixin-de</u> wo.
            he wait-for patiently me
            Intended: "He was waiting for me patiently."

(30) a. Wo <u>jingchang</u> gei wo fuqin xie   xin.
           I   often   to my father write letter
           "I often write letters to my father."

      b. *Wo gei <u>jingchang</u> wo fuqin xie xin.
            I to often my father write letter
            Intended: "I often write letters to my father."

Note that although the Focus Marker can't be inserted immediately in front of an object NP, an object NP may nonetheless be a focused constituent. In that case, the Focus Marker is usually inserted right in front of the verb or the preposition.[9] This point can be seen clearly in (25')–(28'), which differ from the unacceptable sentences in (25)–(28) only in different structural positioning of the Focus Marker.

(25') Ta zai xuexiao <u>shi</u> pengjian-le <u>Zhangsan</u>.

(26') Ta <u>shi</u> bei <u>Zhangsan</u> pian-le.

(27') Ta zai xuexiao <u>shi</u> pengjian-le <u>shei</u>?

(28') Ta <u>shi</u> bei <u>shei</u> pian-le?

3.3 The Effects of Locality Conditions in LF-Movement

With this much about the formal properties of the Chinese Focus Construction in mind, let us now return to the puzzling contrast between (9)–(11) and (12)–(14) raised earlier. (9)–(14) are repeated as (31)–(36) below.

Group A

(31) Shi <u>Zhangsan</u> mai de gou zui ke-ai.
FM Zhangsan buy DE dog cutest
Compare: "*The dog that it is Zhangsan that bought is the cutest."
"It is the dog which was bought by Zhangsan that is the cutest."

(32) Shi <u>shei</u> mai de gou zui ke-ai?
FM who buy DE dog cutest
Compare: "*The dog that who is it that bought is the cutest?"

(33) Wo xiang-zhidao shi <u>shei</u> mai de gou zui ke-ai.
I wonder FM who buy DE dog cutest
Compare: "*I wonder the dog that who is it that bought is the cutest?"

Group B

(34) *wo xihuan shi <u>Zhangsan</u> mai de gou.
I like FM Zhangsan buy DE dog
"*I like the dog that it is Zhangsan that bought."

(35) *Ni xihuan shi <u>shei</u> mai de gou?
you like FM who buy DE dog
"*You like the dog that who it is that bought?"

(36) *Wo xiang-zhidao ni xihuan shi <u>shei</u> mai de gou.
I wonder you like FM who buy DE dog
"*I wonder you like the dog that who it is that bought."

These two groups of sentences differ in an important aspect: the complex NPs in which the focused constituents are embedded occupy the subject position in the acceptable sentences in Group A, while they function as objects in the unacceptable sentences in Group B. Recall the constraint that the formation of Chinese Focus-Construction is subject to. As illustrated above, the Focus Marker *shi* is inserted immediately in front of the focused constituent if the constituent is not an object. If it is a focused object NP, the Focus Marker has to be inserted in front of the verb to avoid coming in between the Case assigner and an assignee of the Accusative. If we assume that what is being focused on is the whole complex NP, as seen in brackets in sentences (1)–(8) above, and not a single constituent embedded in the complex NP, then a straightforward account for this otherwise puzzling contrast is readily available. The reason sentences (34)–(36) are ungrammatical is because they violate the general condition on the formation of the Focus Construction, which prohibits the Focus Marker from being inserted in between a verb or a preposition and an object NP, even when the object NP is a focused constituent. On the other hand, in sentences (31)–(33), the Focus Marker comes right before a subject NP (i.e. the complex NP), and since this is not in violation of the constraint, they are grammatical, as expected. In other words, the contrast between (31)–(33) and (34)–(36) parallels the contrast between (37)–(39) and (40)–(42) below. (34)–(36) are deemed ungrammatical by exactly the same condition that rules out (40)–(42), whereby the latter, containing no complex NPs, clearly has no bearing on the locality conditions in any form.

<u>Group A</u>

(37) [$_{NP}$ Shi <u>Zhangsan</u>] zui ke-ai.
          FM Zhangsan cutest
          "It is Zhangsan that is the cutest."

(38) [$_{NP}$ Shi <u>shei</u>] zui ke-ai?
          FM who cutest
          "Who is it that is the cutest?"

(39) Wo xiang-zhidao [$_{NP}$ shi <u>shei</u>] zui ke-ai.
          I   wonder   FM who cutest
          "I wonder who it is that is the cutest."

<u>Group B</u>

(40) *wo xihuan [$_{NP}$ shi <u>Zhangsan</u>].
          I   like   FM Zhangsan
          Intended: "It is Zhangsan that I like."

(41) *Ni xihuan [$_{NP}$ shi <u>shei</u>]?
    you like   FM who
    Intended: "Who is it that you like?"

(42) *Wo xiang-zhidao ni xihuan [$_{NP}$ shi <u>shei</u>].
    I   wonder   you like   FM who
    Intended: "I wonder who it is that you like."

Note that if we follow Huang in a general sense to assume that a focused constituent, no matter whether a *wh*-phrase or not, undergoes the LF-movement in each of the sentences in (37)–(39), the constituent immediately following the Focus Marker should move to an operator position c-commanding the rest of the sentence, giving rise to the LF-representations in (37')–(39') below.

(37') [[$_{NP}$ Shi <u>Zhangsan</u>]$_i$ [t$_i$ zui ke-ai]].
        FM Zhangsan   cutest

(38') [[$_{NP}$ Shi <u>shei</u>]$_i$ [t$_i$ zui ke-ai]].
        FM who   cutest

(39') Wo xiang-zhidao [$_{NP}$ shi <u>shei</u>]$_i$ [t$_i$ zui ke-ai]].
    I   wonder   FM who   cutest

The same logic applies to the cases of (31)–(33) above, as well. The constituents to be extracted at LF in those sentences will, contrary to what has been widely assumed, be the entire complex NPs, as illustrated in (31'a)–(33'a) and in keeping with Nishigauchi (1985), rather than the single NPs embedded in the complex NPs as in (31'b)–(33'b) below.[10]

(31') a. [[$_{NP}$ Shi <u>Zhangsan</u> mai de gou]$_i$ [t$_i$ zui ke-ai]]
          FM Zhangsan buy DE dog cutest
    b. [[Shi <u>Zhangsan</u>]$_i$ [$_{NP}$ t$_i$ mai de gou] zui ke-ai]]

(32') a. [[$_{NP}$ Shi <u>shei</u> mai de gou]$_i$ [t$_i$ zui ke-ai]]
          FM who buy DE dog   cutest
    b. [[Shi <u>shei</u>]$_i$ [$_{NP}$ t$_i$ mai de gou] zui ke-ai]]

(33') a. Wo xiang-zhidao [[$_{NP}$ Shi <u>shei</u> mai de gou]$_i$ [t$_i$ zui ke-ai]]
      I   wonder   FM who buy DE dog   cutest
    b. Wo xiang-zhidao [[Shi <u>shei</u>]$_i$ [$_{NP}$ t$_i$ mai de gou] zui ke-ai]]

Note now that the LF-movement of the complex NP under this proposal crosses only one bounding node, the S node. Thus it is neither in violation of the Subjacency Condition, nor of any other known locality conditions. We therefore conclude that the LF-movement of argument NPs is fully obedient to the effects of Locality conditions.

If this account for the contrast is correct, then a natural question arises at this point as to whether this analysis can be extended to regular *wh*-questions, like the those in (43)–(45), where there is no insertion of an overt marker *shi*.

(43) [$_{NP}$ <u>shei</u> mai de gou] zui ke-ai?
        who buy DE dog cutest
      Compare: "*The dog that who bought is the cutest?"
      LF: [[$_{NP}$ <u>shei</u> mai de gou]$_i$ [t$_i$ zui ke-ai]]
         who buy DE dog   cutest

(44) Ni xihuan [$_{NP}$ wo piping   <u>shei</u> de wenzhang]?
      you like   I criticize who DE article
      Compare: "*You like the articles in which I criticize who?"
      LF: [[$_{NP}$ wo piping   <u>shei</u> de wenzhang]$_i$ [Ni xihuan t$_i$]]
          I criticize who DE article   you like

(45) Wo xiang-zhidao [$_{NP}$ <u>shei</u> mai de gou] zui ke-ai.
      I   wonder   who buy DE dog cutest
      Compare: "*I wonder the dog that who bought is the cutest?"
      LF: Wo xiang-zhidao[[$_{NP}$ <u>shei</u> mai de gou]$_i$ [t$_i$zui ke-ai]]
         I   wonder   who buy DE dog   cutest

Since there is no overt "marking" in regular *wh*-questions comparable to *shi* in the focus construction, obvious direct evidence for or against this analysis is not very easy to obtain. However, note that conceptually nothing in principle disallows it, given that the terms *wh*-Movement and Focus-Movement are used only as convenient names for two instances of the general rule Move-α. There is no real rule that has to be called *wh*-Movement, but not Focus-Movement, or *vice versa*. The only real rule is the rule Move-α. As instances of Move-α, *wh*-Movement and Focus-Movement, as noted in Huang (1982a/b), each operate on the basis of the feature [+Wh] or [+Focus] respectively. Put differently, it is reasonable, at least conceptually, to assume that in the following simple sentences, the moved elements differ only in their feature bundles but not in the movement rule itself.

(46) Shei da-le ta?
       who beat-Asp him
       "Who beat him?"
       shei: [+Wh; +Human, etc.]

(47) Shi Zhangsan da-le   ta.
       FM Zhangsan beat-Asp him
       "It was Zhangsan that beat him."
       shi Zhangsan: [+Focus; +Human; etc.]

(48) Shi shei da-le ta?
       FM who beat-Asp him
       "Who beat him?"
       shi shei: [+Wh; +Focus; Human; etc.]

In addition to the above conceptual rationale, there are some interesting language facts that, we believe, lend indirect empirical support to this proposal. As is well-known, a *wh*-question like (49a) below can be answered either in full or in short. A full answer, as exemplified in (49b), is basically the repetition of the original question with the *wh*-phrase substituted with a phrase that provides a value for the *wh*-phrase. A short answer, as in (49c), will be the single substituting phrase alone that supplies the minimal information requested, but nothing more than that. There is no answer that is not a repetition of the whole sentence on the one hand, but contains something in addition to the phrase corresponding to the *wh*-phrase, thus, the answer in (49d) is unacceptable. In other words, short answers have to be really short, the deletion of all "unnecessary constituents" is obligatory.

(49) a. Question: <u>Shei</u> mingtian hui lai?
    who tomorrow will come
    "Who will come tomorrow?"

   b. Full Answer: <u>Zhangsan</u> mingtian hui lai.
    Zhangsan tomorrow will come
    "Zhangsan will come tomorrow."

   c. Short Answer: <u>Zhangsan</u>.

   d. Unacceptable Answer: *<u>Zhangsan</u> mingtian.
    Zhangsan tomorrow

Given the general convention that the LF-representation for (49a) is as described in (50), we may naturally generalize this property of short answers as: a legitimate short answer to a *wh*-question can only be a substitute for the constituent that has been raised out and it excludes everything else.

(50) [<u>Shei</u>$_i$ [t$_i$ mingtian hui lai]]
    who tomorrow will come

With this much in mind, let us return to the issue under consideration here. Take (43), repeated as (51a) below, as an example. To provide an answer to this *wh*-question in an appropriate context, one may either give a full answer by repeating the whole sentence with information substituted for the *wh*-phrase, as in (51b), or give a short answer by using a single phrase to provide the minimal information requested as in (51c).

(51) a. Wh-Question: [$_{NP}$ <u>shei</u> mai de gou] zui ke-ai?
    who buy DE dog cutest
    "*The dog that who bought is the cutest?"

   b. Full Answer: [$_{NP}$ <u>Zhangsan</u> mai de gou] zui ke-ai.
    Zhangsan buy DE dog cutest

   c. Short Answer: [$_{NP}$ <u>Zhangsan</u> mai de gou].
    Zhangsan buy DE dog

The fact that (51c) can be a legitimate short answer to a *wh*-question like (51a) is remarkable. Recall the generalization just made above that a legitimate short answer can only be a substitute for the constituent that has been raised out and it excludes everything else. For us, this fact strongly suggests that in *wh*-questions like (51a) what is being LF-moved is not the *wh*-phrase alone, rather it is the whole complex NP in which the *wh*-phrase is embedded, and the LF-Movement, crossing only one bounding node, violates no known locality conditions.

Furthermore, Huang (1982a) appears to share a similar intuition as he remarks that "in (36), (repeated as (52) below) the speaker is, in effect, asking which book, in terms of the identity of the person who is buying it, is the most expensive. In (37) (repeated as (53)) the speaker asks which movie you want to see, in terms of the time when the movie was filmed." However, he does not address the implications on the theory of LF-representations that this crucial semantic property may have. The proposal articulated here, we believe, provides a natural device to capture his important and correct intuition.

(52) [$_{NP}$ Shei yao mai de shu] zui gui?
        who want buy DE book most expensive
        Compare: "*Books that who wants to buy are most
        expensive?"

(53) Ni xiang kan [$_{NP}$ ta shenme shihou pai de dianying]?
        you want see   he   what-time   film DE movie
        Compare: "*You want to see movies that he filmed when?"

It should especially be noted that there may be a question as to why it is always the whole complex NP, but not a constituent within the NP, that is assigned the features [+Wh; +Focus; etc.] and undergoes the LF-movement. This is a nontrivial question, especially when we note that the constituent that carries the feature [+Wh] appears, at least superficially, to be the *wh*-phrase alone and not the whole complex NP containing the *wh*-phrase in the *wh*-questions above, and that the constituent that is focused upon (thus carrying the feature [+Focus]) also can be a constituent within the complex NP and not the complex NP as a whole. Put differently, there may be two questions: (i) Does a constituent have to carry the feature [+Wh] or [+Focus] for the LF-movement to apply to it; and (ii) if the answer to (i) is positive, how does a constituent like a complex NP, which may not have such features in the first place, obtain such feature(s) at a later point in the course of a derivation?

As for question (i), it is reasonable to assume that the answer is yes. As a general syntactic rule, Move-α is supposed to operate quite freely. But some initial motivation for its application seems to be necessary. Features such as [+Wh] and [+Focus] and so on often provide such a motivation. This point can be made even stronger when we interpret the *wh*-Criterion (Aoun, Hornstein, and Sportiche (1981)) in a broad sense, with an effect that requires a feature match between a syntactic position and a syntactic constituent that terminates in that position. Thus, it is natural to assume that the constituent ending up in a certain position, rather than just a part of the constituent, has a feature match with the position.

Regarding question (ii), we follow Nishgauchi (1985) and assume that there are two steps of LF-movement involved in the LF derivation of the sentences under consideration. At the first step, the constituent with [+Wh] (i.e. the *wh*-phrase) or a constituent with the feature [+Focus] moves to a COMP position of the relative clause within the complex NP, and the moved element in its new position has its features percolated up to the complex NP probably through an intermediate node S'. As a result of this movement and feature percolation, the complex NP obtains the features [+Wh; +Focus; etc]. The second step of LF-movement applies to raise the complex NP with the features [+Wh; +Focus; etc.] to a matrix COMP position. This point can be illustrated with examples (54) (= (31)) and (55) (= (43)) as follows.

(54) [NP Shi <u>Zhangsan</u> mai de gou] zui ke-ai.
      FM Zhangsan buy DE dog cutest
      Compare: "*The dog that it is Zhangsan that bought is the cutest."

(54') a. STEP 1

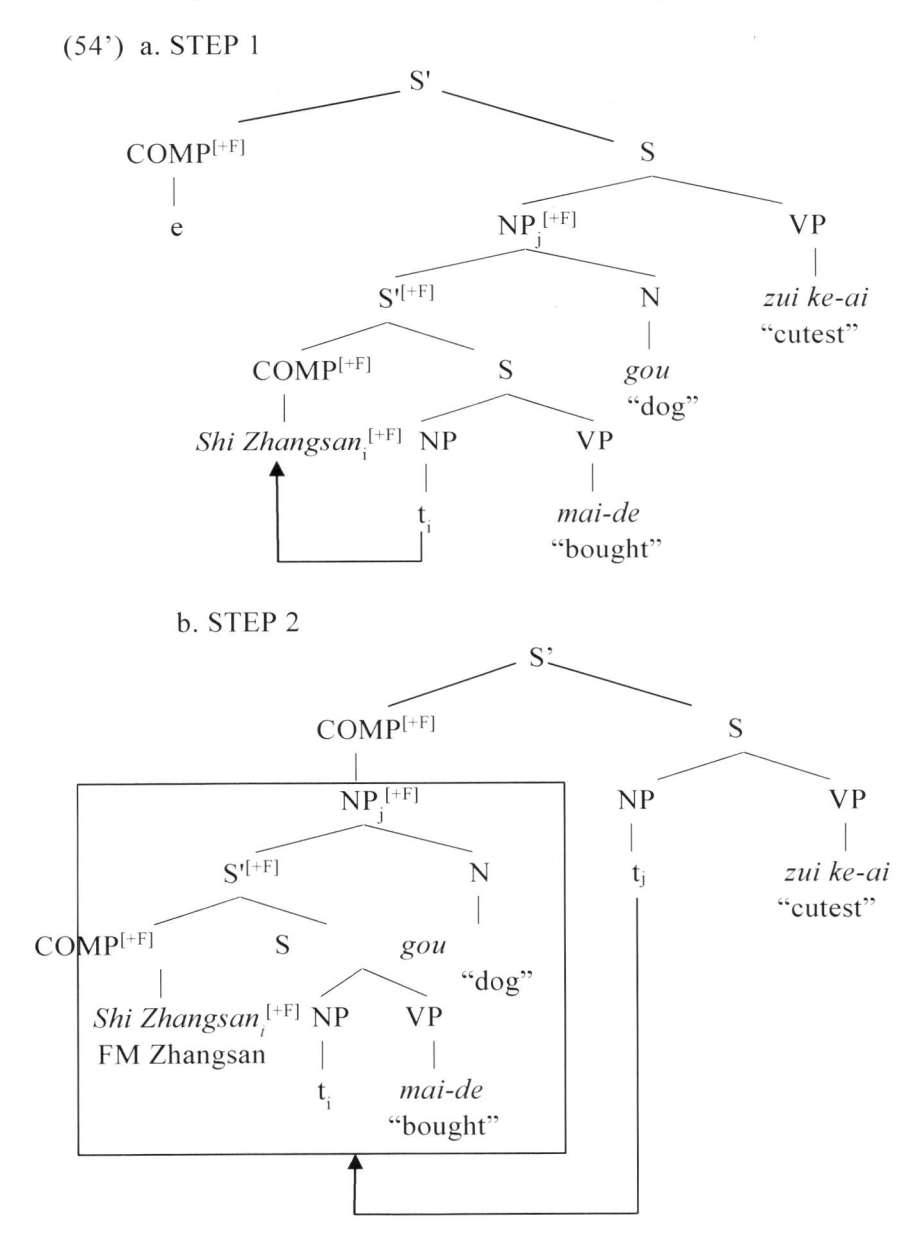

b. STEP 2

(55) [NP <u>Shei</u> mai de gou] zui ke-ai?
     who buy DE dog cutest
    Compare: "*The dog that who bought is the cutest?"

(55') a. STEP 1

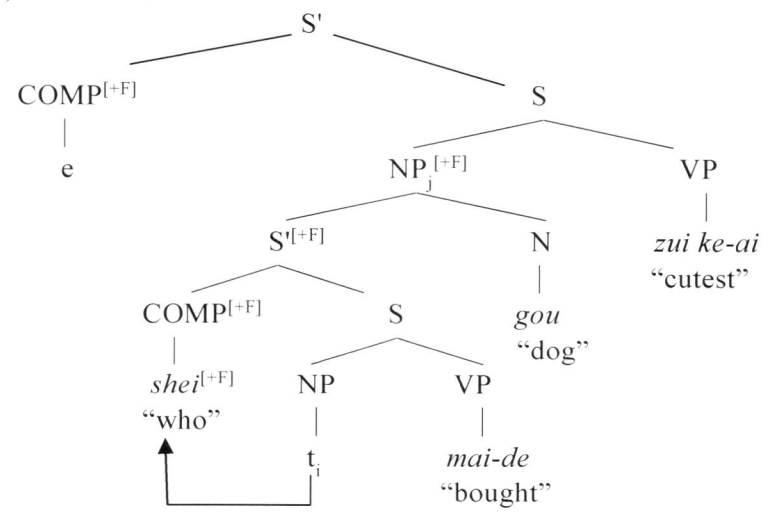

    b. STEP 2

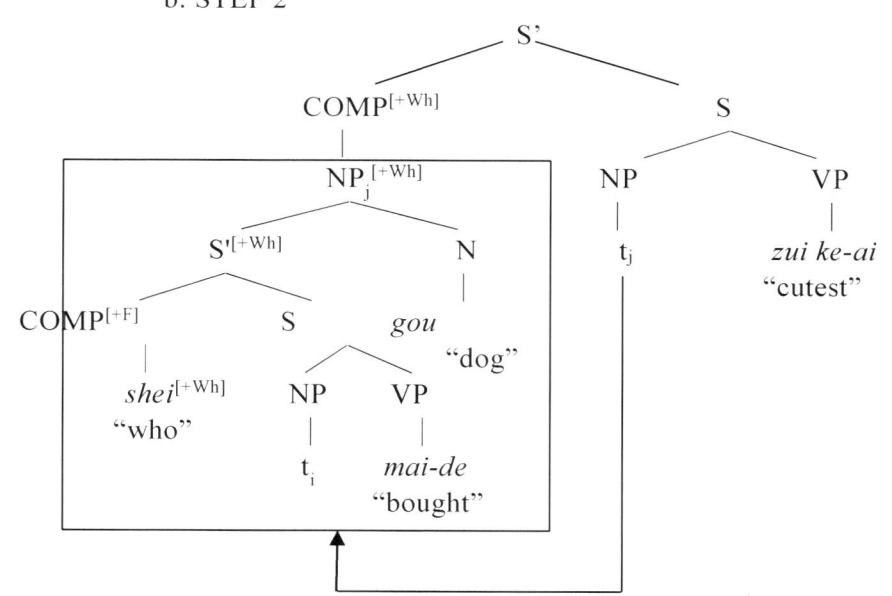

Finally, it should be pointed out that although the formation of *wh*-questions and that of the focus construction in Chinese do not involve the overt dislocation of any constituent in Syntax, an NP moves upward to a sentence initial position in Topic construction. We note that only a whole complex NP, but not any constituent embedded within the NP, may undergo such an NP-movement. We would interpret this phenomenon as an additional piece of supporting evidence for the proposal articulated in this chapter.

(56) a. [$_{NP}$ wo piping <u>shei</u> de wenzhang]$_i$ ni xihuan t$_i$?
   I criticize who DE article   you like
   Compare: "*You like articles in which I criticize who?"

   b. *[shei]$_i$ ni xihuan wo piping t$_i$ de wenzhang?
   Who you like I criticize DE article
   Compare: "*You like articles in which I criticize who?"

(57) a. [$_{NP}$ <u>shi shei</u> mai de gou]$_i$ ni xihuan t$_i$?
   FM who buy DE dog you like
   Compare: "*Do you like the dog that who is it that bought?"

   b. *[<u>Shi</u> shei]$_i$ ni xihuan t$_i$ mai de gou ?
   FM who you like buy DE dog
   Compare: "*Do you like the dog that who is it that bought?"

3.4 Summary

This article started with a brief discussion of the problems with Huang's proposal concerning LF-movement in Chinese. We have found that for Huang's approach, there is a puzzling contrast systematically observed between two types of sentences involving apparent violations of the Subjacency condition in the LF-movement of argument NPs.[11] We have proposed an account for this contrast and demonstrated that the contrast has nothing to do with locality conditions, and that it is due to a fundamental property of the Chinese Focus Construction and to the general condition on the positioning of the Chinese Focus marker *shi*.

It has also been demonstrated, more interestingly, that this explanation suggests an interesting way of looking at the issues that have been considered by many authors, but have not received a satisfactory treatment: In the LF-derivation of the sentences involving apparent violations of the Subjacency condition, the *wh*-phrase, the focused constituent, and the focused *wh*-phrase do not raise out of the complex NP; rather, they move only within the relative clause. As a consequence of this movement process, the features [+Wh; +Focus; etc.] associated with the moved elements percolate up to the entire complex NP, which in turn trigger the movement of the entire complex NP to an operator position. That is to say that in Chinese, Pied-Piping in LF is very much in line with what is proposed in Nishigauchi (1985). We conclude that the LF-movement of argument NPs, just like the syntactic movement of argument NPs, is under the constraint of the relevant locality conditions.

Notes

[1] Logical Form (LF), which is a syntactic representation, specifies linguistically determined aspects of meaning (Chomsky and Lasnik (1995)).

[2] "Locality condition" (or "Subjacency Condition" as alternatively termed) refers generally to a range of syntactic conditions on construct derivation (i.e. conditions on transformational operations) and representations (i.e. licensing conditions). For instance, no constituent can be moved out of two or more containing NP/S-nodes in any single rule application, and a constituent in a certain position cannot be related to another constituent in another position if the two positions are technically too far away from each other. Complex Noun Phrase Constraint (CNPC), being subsumed under this general condition, specifies a condition as follows.

> No rule can move any element out of a Complex Noun Phrase Clause (i.e. no rule can move any constituent X out of the bracketed clause in any structure of the following type (i)) (Radford (1981)).
>
> (i) $[_{NP} ... N - [_{S'} ... X ...] ...]$

[3] The Chinese copular verb *shi* has two major functions: Equation (just like its English counterpart "be") and emphasis. Syntactically, *shi* in emphatic usage takes up a pre-verbal or a pre-adjective position, functioning very much like an adverbial. See Xu (2001) for a detailed discussion about the point.

[4] Lexical INFL Hypothesis is proposed by Huang (1982b) to capture a number of Chinese facts: (1) absence of *that*-trace effects; (2) long-distance reflexives; (3) non-gap topic (e.g. *Shuiguo. wo xihuan pingguo.* '(As for) fruits, I like apples.'); and (4) topic chain (null topic). Xu (2003) argues that functional categories are functional universally, and that the above language facts can be recast and properly derived by independently motivated principles without revoking the Lexical INFL Hypothesis.

[5] Adjuncts in Chinese, under Huang's assumption, are adjoined to VPs, thus they are neither lexically governed by the verb (government blocked by the lower VP node), nor lexically governed by INFL (government blocked by the higher adjoined VP node).

[6] Phonetic Form (PF) as a level of linguistic representation specifies linguistically determined aspects of sound (Chomsky and Lasnik (1995)).

[7] Since the literature on which this study is based were conducted in rather traditional frameworks, we use the traditional terms, such as S and S' instead of IP and CP throughout this chapter. We believe that the general claims made here can be easily translated into the new framework of grammar without affecting the essential contents.

[8] Lebeaux (1991) defines 'Adjoin-α' in a very general way, referring to a syntactic operation that works to get a syntactic element inserted in a certain position of a phrase marker. Furthermore, Adjoin-α, Move-α, and Project- α are all subsumed under an even more generalized conception 'Affect-α', according to Lebeaux (1991). A slightly different version of such a conception is taken up by Chomsky and Lasnik (1995), who claim that the transformational operations are movement (adjunction and substitution), deletion, and insertion, which are all instances of the general operation Affect-α, α being arbitrary.

[9] Note also that in cases in which the Focus Marker *shi* is inserted in front of a verb, the sentence may be ambiguous, since the verb may itself be a focused constituent. The following sentence, for example, may have two possible readings with respect to focus. In one reading, Zhangsan *rents* (as opposed to buying) this house; while in the other, Zhangsan rents *this house* (rather than other houses).

(i) Zhangsan shi zu zhedong fangzi.
    Zhangsan FM rent this house.

[10] Fiengo, Huang, Lasnik, and Reinhart (1989) note that there are theoretical and empirical problems with Nishigaochi's (1985) LF Pied-Piping approach.

For instance, some superiority facts cannot be properly explained under the hypothesis, and more importantly, the LF Pied-Piping Hypothesis does not seem to be applicable to the whole range of island violations in LF. We interpret those arguments against the LF Pied-Piping Hypothesis as consequences of an obvious overgeneralization to such an extent that all the Subjacency-violating constructions are interpreted as resulting from LF Pied-Piping. The situation is much more complicated than Nishigauchi (1985) assumes it to be. A distinction among different types of Subjacency-violating constructions has to be carefully made. While some of them may have resulted from LF Pied-Piping, others perhaps have not. However, the facts about the Chinese Focus Construction presented in this chapter show that this kind of apparent Subjacency-violating construction should fall under the category in which the LF Pied-Piping takes place.

[11] In this chapter, we do not concern ourselves with the problems of the effects of locality conditions in the LF-movement of adjuncts like *weishenme* 'why' and *zenme* 'how'. We will explore the relevant issues in another paper.

Chapter 4

Two Types of Null Subject Languages[*]

ABSTRACT: *In this chapter, it is argued that the Chinese-type I (INFL) and the English-type I behave contrastively in assigning Nominative Case to the Spec position of an IP. In the former, Nominative Case assignment is optional and only assigned when there is a lexical NP in the subject position that needs such a Case assignment. It does not require Nominative Case assignment, thus allowing null subjects. In contrast, the English-type I must assign Nominative Case, thus requiring an (either semantic or expletive) NP or its equivalent in the subject position to discharge the assignment, disallowing null subjects in principle. We demonstrate that this minimal assumption provides a straightforward account of the contrast between the Chinese-type languages that permit null subjects and the English-type languages that don't. As for languages like Italian and Spanish, which permit null subjects on one hand, but exhibit rich inflectional morphology (an English-type I) on the other, we argue that the rich I in those languages contains a pronominal element. This element is similar to a CP, a clitic, or an expletive pronoun, in that it may discharge the obligatory Nominative Case assignment in the place of a lexical NP, although such an element does not require a Case assignment. In other words, there exist two types of null subjects cross-linguistically, and Italian permits null subjects for fundamentally*

[*]A version of this chapter originally appeared with the same title in Jie Xu, Donghong Ji, and Kim Teng Lua (eds.) *Chinese Syntax and Semantic*, 2003, Singapore and London: Prentice Hall, pp. 257–280. Revisions made are technical and minimal, the essential contents remain unchanged. It is included in this monograph as a chapter with kind permission from the Pearson Education Asia, Singapore.

> *different reasons from Chinese. According to our proposal, it is expected*
> *that the property of null subjects clusters with different sets of properties*
> *in different types of null subject languages. We argue that the optional*
> *vs. obligatory assignments of Nominative Case represent only partial*
> *effects of a much more general UG principle, the "Generalized Case*
> *Filter" (GCF), which is a principled specification of a bi-directional and*
> *mutual dependency between Case assigners and assignees.*

4.0 Introduction: Two Types of INFL

The nature of <u>INFL</u> (INFLection) in the Chinese-type languages is fundamentally different from that in the English-type languages. In Xu (1993), we have proposed and argued that this difference is a result of the setting of a single, two-valued parameter, the <u>I</u>-Parameter. If the parameter is fixed in the English way (<u>Ie</u>), the <u>I</u> as the functional head of a sentence will contain three elements: [Tense] [Agr] [Predicator]. If the parameter is set in the Chinese way (<u>Ic</u>), the <u>I</u> has only the phonetically null functional category [Predicator] as its content. We have also argued that the Chinese setting of the <u>I</u>-Parameter represents a default and unmarked option, which may be the initial value specified in UG, and thus attainable in advance of any linguistic experience. The fact that children acquiring the Chinese language fix the parameter is due to the absence of the required trigger (inflectional morphology) that would have induced a different setting. Taking it a step further, we assert that the parameters whose setting can occur only with morphological properties, such as triggers, will all be assigned a UG-given, default value in languages like Chinese that have little or no morphology.

Pursuing the general approach along which a single parameter setting may result in many superficial differences between languages, in Xu (1993) we have conducted an extensive investigation of the consequences that the setting of this parameter may lead to in the theory of grammar. The two specific roles played by <u>I</u>, as natural results of the development of Case theory and of extended X-bar theory, are to assign abstract Nominative Case and to head a syntactic projection. We have argued that differently valued I's behave contrastively in the ways in which they select their complements and Case-mark the NPs in their Spec. These two types of contrast are quite general with wide-ranging effects, and subsume several important typological differences that an optimal theory of grammar must capture. We have argued, for example, that I<u>e</u> only selects a VP as its complement because in this type of language, V must ultimately head a projection governed by I in order to receive tense and agreement information (Roberts (1985), and Larson (1988), among others). By contrast, the only selectional condition placed on its complements by I<u>c</u> is the feature [+Predicative], essentially a feature match between a [Predicator] head and its [Predicative] complement. So in I<u>c</u> languages, AP, NP, PP, and even IP, as well as VP can be the complements of an I<u>c</u>, since they all have the feature [+Predicative]. In the case where an IP happens to be a complement of a higher I<u>c</u>, a sentence apparently seems to have two NPs in a pre-verbal position (the outer one is normally termed "topic"). According to our analysis, the two NPs each take an independent Spec/IP position, with the linearly-ordered outer one being in the Spec of the matrix IP and the inner one in the Spec of an embedded IP. Thus formal-syntactically speaking, "topics" are "subjects." Along this line of approach, the effects assumed under the so-called "Topic Constructions," "Multiple Nominative Constructions," "Topic-/Subject-Prominent Language Typology," and "Discourse-/Sentence-Oriented Language Typology" are all naturally explained in a principled way, without invoking any ad hoc stipulations. The Topic mark observed in languages like Korean and Japanese, we argue, is not itself a Case Mark. Rather, it is assigned on completely different grounds, and may override a Nominative Case marking, preventing the latter from surfacing at PF.

Please note that the NP in the Spec/IP is assigned the abstract Case of Nominative by I. It is also generally assumed that the assignment takes place through "Spec-Head agreement." We assume that this is a UG-specified property of human languages, which holds cross-linguistically.

(1)

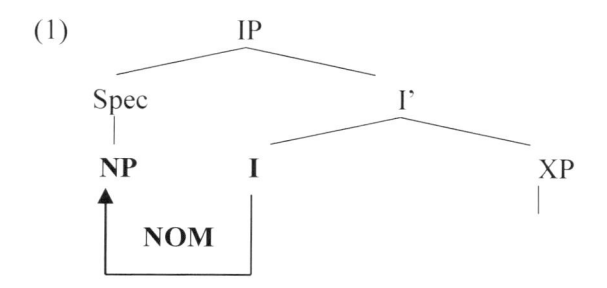

Given the I-parameter articulated in Xu (1993), it makes sense to ask whether I's fixed at different values behave contrastively in assigning Nominative Case. In this chapter we argue that they do, and that their different behaviors in assigning Nominative Case give rise to several typological distinctions.

4.1 Null Subjects in Ic Languages

We would like to claim here that Ie, but not Ic, is obligated to assign the abstract Nominative Case. So not only can the functional head I in English-type languages assign Nominative Case, it must do so. This requires the presence of a lexical NP, or something else, to discharge (receive) the Case assignment. We attribute the contrast between the *a* and *b* sentences below to the requirement that Ie assign Nominative Case. In particular, it is because the obligatory assignment is discharged to a lexical NP that the sentences under *a* are well-formed, while failure to discharge the Case assignment in *b* causes those sentences to be ungrammatical. It does not matter whether the semantic content can be understood, an overt NP has to be placed there to discharge the Case assignment.

(2) a. [$_{NP}$ John] Ie bought a book.

b. *[e] Ie Bought a book.

(3) a. [$_{NP}$ They] Ie will come.

b. *[e] Ie Will come.

(4) a. [$_{NP}$ He] Ie likes apples.

b. *[e] Ie Likes apples.

(5) a. [$_{NP}$ Mary] Ie was planning to come over.

    b. *[e] Ie was planning to come over.

(6) a. [$_{NP}$ Bill and Jill] Ie worked in Singapore for ten years.

    b. *[e] Ie worked in Singapore for ten years.

Even though there is no semantic subject, an expletive pronoun like *it* or *there*, as a dummy subject, has to be inserted to discharge the obligatory assignment of Nominative Case.

(7) a. [$_{NP}$ It] Ie is raining.

    b. *[e] Ie Is raining.

(8) a. [$_{NP}$ There] Ie is a book on the table.

    b. *[e] Ie Is a book on the table.

It should be noted that, although it is usually an NP that discharges the obligatory Case assignment, it does not have to be an NP. For example, the clausal category CP, although not requiring a Case assignment for itself, may also discharge the obligatory assignment, saving a sentence from Case violation. The patterning of grammaticality of the sentences in (9) below is remarkable: CP and NP, of course, contrast in that the latter but not the former requires a Case assignment. A CP is allowed to occur in a Caseless position like that of the object of a passivized verb where an NP is excluded, thus the contrast between *a* and *b* in (9). These two types of syntactic categories, nevertheless, pattern similarly in their capacity of discharging the obligatory Case assignment. Therefore, *c* and *d* of (9) are equally acceptable in contrast with (9e), in which the obligatory assignment of Nominative is not discharged to either an NP or a CP.

(9) a.*It is believed [$_{NP}$ the man].

    b. It is believed [$_{CP}$ that the space shuttle flies very high].

    c. [$_{NP}$ The space shuttle] Ie is amazing.

    d. [$_{CP}$ That the space shuttle flies so high] Ie is amazing.

    e.*[e] Ie Is amazing.

Turning now to the <u>Ic</u> languages, given their distinctive feature concerning null subjects, it is not unreasonable to assume that the assignment of Nominative Case by <u>Ic</u> is optional in the sense that it applies only when it is needed. That is, when some NP needs to receive a Case assignment. Crucially, it does not have to apply if there is no NP that needs such an assignment, thus not requiring a discharge. In short, the proposal about the contrast between <u>Ie</u> and <u>Ic</u> concerning their Case assigning property can be schematized as in (10) and (11) respectively.

(10) Obligatory Assignment of Nominative Case in Ie Languages

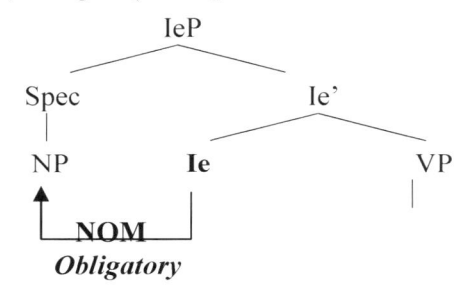

(11) Optional Assignment of Nominative Case in Ic Languages

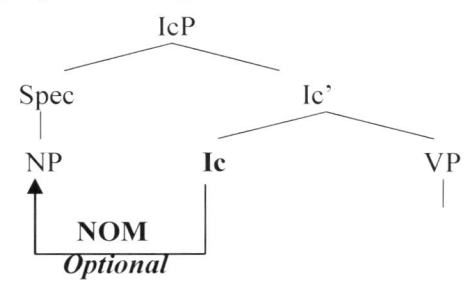

As one of the immediate consequences resulting from the optional nature of <u>Ic</u> Nominative Case assignment, <u>Ic</u> languages, sharply contrasting with <u>Ie</u> languages, permit the so-called "null subjects." For the same reason, no expletive pronouns comparable to English *it* and *there* are necessary in this type of language. In fact, they cannot be used if we follow the spirit of the general proposal of the Principle of Licensing Well-Formedness (UG) (Lebeaux (1991)), assuming that a category cannot appear in a phrase marker unless and until it is licensed. It is the Case discharge requirement and nothing else that licenses expletive pronouns. So, the *a* sentences with lexical NPs and the *b* sentences without in (12)–(14) are equally well-formed in Chinese.

(12) a. [$_{NP}$ Zhangsan] <u>Ic</u> mai le yi ben shu.
     Zhangsan buy Asp one CL book
     "Zhangsan bought a book."

    b. [e] <u>Ic</u> mai le yi ben shu.
     buy Asp one CL book
     "(Someone) bought a book."

(13) a. [$_{NP}$ Tamen] <u>Ic</u> hui lai.
     they will come
     "They will come. "

    b. [e] <u>Ic</u> hui lai.
     will come
     "(Someone) will come."

(14) a. [$_{NP}$ Ta] <u>Ic</u> xihuan pinguo.
     he like apple
     "He likes apples."

    b. [e] <u>Ic</u> xihuan pingguo.
     Like apple
     "(Someone) likes apples."

From a formal syntactic viewpoint, the use of null subjects is, in principle, absolutely free in <u>Ic</u> languages, although a lexical NP in some cases may be preferable over an empty category for pragmatic purposes such as clarity, emphasis, and avoidance of ambiguity. Whether an overt NP is needed in the subject position is determined by factors other than formal syntax. The formal syntax simply does not have conditions governing the use of null subjects. With regard to null subjects, we may picture the formal syntax of <u>Ic</u>-languages as saying: If you need an NP in the subject position for some reason, feel free use one and a Nominative Case will be assigned to it. If you don't, that is also fine!" Note also that although this chapter mainly discusses Chinese, the principle carries over nicely to Korean and Japanese, as those two Ic-languages also allow relatively free use of null subjects and don't have expletive pronouns.

Note that it is a crucial assumption for our proposal that the assignment of abstract Case can be either optional or obligatory. A more general formulation of these phenomena will be provided later; however, we here note that this assumption is not another artifact that we make just for our purposes. Rather, it is a part of a much more general cross-structural phenomenon that demands an appropriate form of representation in the theory of grammar. Another representative case for optional Case assignment, for example, is the Genitive. The assignment of Genitive Case is optional, perhaps universally. A head noun is capable of assigning Genitive Case to an NP in its Spec if there is an NP that needs such assignment, but it does not require a discharge, thus permitting "null Spec/NP." The following pairs of sentences suffice to illustrate this point.

(A) English

(15) a. I like [$_{NP}$ John's] books.

    b. I like [e] books.

(B) Chinese

(16) a. Wo xihuan [$_{NP}$ Zhangsan-de shu].
       I like Zhangsan-DE book]
       "I like Zhangsan's books."

    b. Wo xihuan [e] shu]
       I like book
       "I like books."

Obligatory Case assignment, the other extreme, can be observed in the assignment of Accusative Case by prepositions in both Chinese and English. This is particularly clear from the contrast between the *a* and *b* sentences in (17) and (18).

(A) English

(17) a. John will go to the campus with [$_{NP}$ me].

    b.*John will go to the campus with [e].

(B) Chinese

(18) a. Zhangsan hui gen [$_{NP}$ wo] qu xuexiao.
      Zhangsan will with [me] go campus
      "Zhangsan will go to the campus with [me]."

    b. *Zhangsan hui gen [e] qu xuexiao.
      Zhangsan will with go campus
      Intended: "Zhangsan will go to campus with (with somebody)."

4.2 Two Sources for Null Subjects

The proposal suggested above not only offers a straightforward account of the contrast between null-subject and non-null-subject languages (henceforth, "NS and NNS languages"), but also captures the long-noted intuition that the null-subject phenomena should be somehow related to overt morphological inflections in a principled way. However, this proposal appears to run into problems when one takes broader language diversity into consideration. As noted extensively in the literature (e.g. Rizzi (1982), Zagona (1982), Huang (1984a and 1984b), Burzio (1986), and Hyams (1989)), the Romance languages have rich inflections, but also manifest null subject phenomenon. This is a problem for our proposal because the I-Parameter must have been fixed in the English way (Ie), so that the assignment of Nominative in those languages should be obligatory, demanding a discharge and disallowing null subjects just as in English. Consider the following data (due to Burzio (1986) for Italian and Huang (1984a and 1984b) for Spanish).

(A) Italian

(19) [e] ved-e Maria.
     sees Maria
     "(He) sees Maria."

(B) Spanish

(20) Jose sabe que [e] ha sido visto por Maria.
     Jose know that [e] has been seen by Maria
     "Jose knows that (he) has been seen by Maria."

If it is correct to assume that the I-Parameter in Italian and Spanish is fixed at the value of Ie, and must assign the Nominative Case, then the question is how the obligatory Case assignment is discharged. To solve this problem, we would follow a general proposal characterized in various forms in the works of Rizzi (1982), Zagona (1982), Burzio (1986) and Hyams (1989), and assume that the enriched I in those languages contains a particular kind of pronominal element. We propose that this pronominal element, like the expletives *it* and *there*, clitics, and CP, may serve to discharge a Case assignment, although it does not require one. The English I, presumably because of the language's degenerate inflectional morphology, does not contain such an element, and so an expletive must be inserted as an alternative. Thus there exists a contrast between the Italian- and English-type languages in the occurrence of null subjects, although both language types have Ie that contrasts with Chinese Ic. It should also be noted that the pronominal element's discharge of the Case assignment is optional (and so is that of CP). That is to say, it operates only if the latter cannot be discharged otherwise. If there is an NP already in the subject position, the pronominal element will not have to do so. That is why null subjects may alternate with lexical ones in those languages.

(A) Italian

(21) a. [e] ved-e Maria.
        sees Maria
        "(He) sees Maria."

     b. Giovanni ved-e Maria.
        Giovanni see-s Maria
        "Giovanni sees Maria."

(B) Spanish

(22) a. Jose sabe que [e] ha sido visto por Maria.
      Jose know that has been seen by Maria
      "Jose knows that (he) has been seen by Maria."

  b. Jose sabe que el ha sido visto por Maria.
     Jose know that he has been seen by Maria
     "Jose knows that he has been seen by Maria."

This proposal amounts to claiming that two sources exist for null subjects, and that languages may have null subjects for two fundamentally different reasons: one is due to the optional assignment of Nominative Case; the other to the availability of a pronominal element. The Case is not assigned at all in the former case, while in the latter it has been discharged to an element this is not a lexical NP. This treatment of null subjects probably represents a nontrivial departure from the previous theories, thus demanding some further comments.

First, please note that this proposal is a desirable one conceptually since it provides a natural explanation for an interesting (and correct, I believe) observation made in Huang (1984a/b) that the phenomenon of null subjects can occur when there is a rich agreement element in a language, or when there is no agreement at all. This observation is true descriptively, but given this odd state of affairs, the question is why that should be the case. Now we see that a language with rich agreement may have null subjects because its agreement system may contain a pronominal element that is capable of discharging Case assignment. A language with no agreement at all may have null subjects because the language fixes the I-parameter at I_c, which assigns Nominative Case optionally, and does not require a discharge.

Second, as noted in the literature (e.g. Li and Thompson (1976)), in the Chinese-type languages the null subject phenomenon is not an isolated property. Rather, it always clusters with other formal properties, such as AP/NP predicates, "the Topic Construction," "multiple Nominative Constructions," and subject anaphors. There are good reasons to believe that those properties are associated in some way, since they cluster in many different languages like Chinese, Korean and Japanese. Those properties that cluster with the null subject phenomenon, to my knowledge, are not attested in the Italian-type languages, which raises many questions. This otherwise curious discrepancy, if our general proposal on the I-Parameter articulated in this book is correct, is expected, given that null subjects and other related properties are all derivable from the nature of I in the Chinese-type NS languages only but not in the Italian-type NS languages.

Third, as argued by Rizzi (1982) and Burzio (1986), among others, quite convincingly, the null subject property is intrinsically related to the free subject inversion property in the Italian-type languages. Consider some examples from Italian (Burzio (1986)).

(23) a. Giovanni telefon-a.
      Giovanni telephone-s
      "Giovanni telephones."

    b. [e] telefon-a Giovanni.
      telephone-s Giovanni
      "Giovanni telephones."

(24) a. Maria e arrivata.
      Maria is arrived(fem.)
      "Maria has arrived."

    b. [e] e arrivata Maria.
      is arrived(fem.) Maria
      "Maria has arrived."

According to Rizzi and Burzio, free inversion is possible in Italian because null subjects are possible in the language. The null subject position gets assigned Nominative Case first and then it transmits the Case to the inverted subject (i.e. i-subject) in accordance with Case and theta role assignment conditions. In the words of Burzio (1986), the complete productivity of inversion in Italian is a reflex of the null-subject property, the former is strictly contingent on the latter. Note that if Chinese allows null subjects for the same reason, then we would expect Chinese to be like Italian in allowing free inversion. But, in fact, free inversion is not generally possible in the language.

(25) a. Zhangsan da dianhua le.
   Zhangsan make phone-call Asp
   "Zhangsan made a phone call."

  b. *da dianhua le Zhangsan.
   make phone-call Asp Zhangsan

(26) a. Lisi hui lai.
   Lisi will come
   "Lisi will come."

  b. *hui lai Lisi.
   will come Lisi

This contrast between Chinese and Italian, two NS languages, would present a problem if the inversion property followed from the null-subject property, and if null subjects were possible in Chinese and Italian for the same reasons. This problem disappears under our proposal. Note that a simple account for this contrast is readily available if we assume, with Burzio, that the null subject, after receiving a Nominative Case from $\underline{I}$, transmits the Case to the post-verbal i-subject so that the subject can be inverted.[1] The Chinese subject cannot be inverted because Case transmission does not occur in the language. Recall our assumption that the assignment of Nominative by $\underline{Ic}$ is optional, applying only when there is a lexical NP in the pre-verbal subject position that needs a Case assignment. In sentences (25b) and (26b) the subject position is simply empty, so the assignment of Nominative does not take place, hence no Case will be transmitted to the inverted subject, yielding a lexical NP in a Caseless position. Contrastively, in Italian $\underline{Ie}$ must assign the Nominative Case regardless of whether the pre-verbal subject position is empty or fulfilled. If it is fulfilled by a lexical NP, the lexical NP takes up the Case assignment; if empty, the Case may either be discharged by a pronominal element (in the case of null subjects) or be transmitted to another NP with which it is co-indexed (in the case of inverted subjects).

Finally, the use of null subjects is subject to different conditions in the two types of NS languages. In the Chinese-type NS languages, there are no syntactic conditions on the occurrence of null subjects, since they are determined by semantic and/or pragmatic factors. In contrast, the use of null subjects in the other type of languages is tied to the presence of agreement Inflections. For example, a finite verb may or may not show agreement in Arabic, but a subject may drop only when the verb shows agreement. This probably holds true in the Italian-type NS languages as well.

4.3 Deriving "the Null Subject Parameter"

With respect to the nature of null subjects (and empty pronouns in general), recent work in generative grammar has devoted considerable attention to the issue of which parameter(s) of UG enable languages to differ in precisely the ways that they do, formulating "the Pro-Drop Parameter" or "the Null-Subject Parameter" (see Chomsky (1981), Huang (1984a/b), Jaeggli (1982), Jaeggli and Safir (1989), Rizzi (1982), Taraldsen (1978), among many others). One important type of explanation that has been proposed in the literature to distinguish "non-pro-drop" languages like English and French and "pro-drop" languages like Italian and Spanish is based on the idea of recoverability and the observation, due originally to Taraldsen (1978), that the possibility of pro-drop in a language often correlates with the existence of a rich INFLectional morphology, in particular a rich system of agreement. Following this approach, Italian and Spanish allow a pronoun to drop from the subject position of a tensed clause because there is a rich system of subject-verb agreement in these languages. The agreement marking on a verb is rich enough to determine, or recover, the content of a missing subject; therefore, such a missing subject is allowed. On the other hand, the agreement system of English and French are somewhat degenerate, and the agreement marking on a verb is too meager to identify the content of a missing subject, so subjects may not drop. Thus the null subject parameter, in the words of Rizzi (1982), reduces to properties of the verbal Inflection system: in Italian, "strong" agreement (Agr) licenses **pro** subjects; in French or English, the "weaker" agreement does not. However, Huang (1984a), based on the evidence from Chinese, Korean and Japanese, correctly notes that this approach may be right for some reasons, but must be wrong for others, since it predicts that the Chinese-type languages would not allow null subjects. The situation, in fact, is precisely the opposite, for these languages apparently allow "pro-drop" even more freely than those with rich agreement systems.

In an interesting attempt to solve the problem, Huang (1984a/b) developed a disjunctive approach, along which the relevant facts may be derived jointly by (a) the principle of recoverability, (b) the assumption that a zero pronoun is a pronoun, (c) the assumption that agreement marking on Agr on a verb qualifies as potential "antecedent" of a zero pronoun, and (d) the Generalized Control Rule (GCR). In this way, Huang claims that he derives the effects of the Pro-Drop Parameter. Setting his discussions of the empty object aside, some of Huang's examples are as follow.

(27) a. [e] came.

b. John said that [e] saw Bill.

c. John tried [e] to come.

Sentences in the form of (27c) are well-formed in all of the three language types (Chinese, English, and Italian). (27a) and (27b) are also well-formed in Chinese and Italian, but not in English. Based on Huang's proposal, they are ill-formed in English because Agr, which is the closest nominal element, is too meager to determine the content of the missing subject. In contrast, these two sentences are well-formed in Italian because the Agr in those languages is rich enough to determine the content of the missing subject. (27a) is grammatical in Chinese because it is a variable bound to a discourse topic, and (27b) is well-formed because the closest nominal is *John* (there being no Agr), which can recover its content. This mode of explanation seems to be promising because it is capable of capturing the facts from the three types of languages.

However, there is a nontrivial problem with it. Consider the two pairs of English sentences in (28) and (29). Although Huang (1984a/b) can account for the contrast between (28a) and (28b) by saying that sentence (28a) has a missing subject and its Agr is too meager to determine its content, yielding a recoverability violation, it cannot explain the contrast between sentences (29a), which has a null subject, and (29b), which has a semantically empty expletive, since sentence (29a) has no missing subject with lexical content to be determined, but is, nevertheless, ungrammatical.

(28) a. *[e] came.

    b. John came.

(29) a. *[e] is raining.

    b. It is raining.

For the proposal we have provided in this chapter, the contrast between (28a) and (28b) is of exactly the same type as that between (29a) and (29b). The ill-formed sentences under (a) in both pairs are pure violations of the Case discharge requirement, rather than the non-syntactic recoverability principle. Moreover, our approach is also capable of deriving the desirable language effects with respect to null subjects, consequently deriving the Pro-Drop Parameter itself, from independently motivated and generalized principles of UG without invoking the assumptions that Huang must assume, namely the I-parameter and an assumption that obligatory assignment of Nominative Case can be discharged to quite diverse types of categories. We would also like to argue that the discharge of obligatory assignment of Nominative is simply a special instance of a general requirement of Case discharge, which we will present below.

It is also worthwhile noting a newer version of the "Null Subject Parameter" proposed in Jaeggli and Safir (1989). Attempting to provide a unified account for different types of null subject languages, Jaeggli and Safir introduce the notion of "Morphological Uniformity." Their proposal goes as follows.

(30) a. The Null Subject Parameter (NSP)
Null subjects are permitted in all and only languages with morphologically uniform Inflectional paradigms.

    b. Morphological Uniformity (MU)
An inflectional paradigm P in a language L is morphologically uniform iff P has either only un-derived Inflectional forms or only derived Inflectional forms.

By "the languages with un-derived Inflectional forms," they mean the languages of the Chinese-type; and by "the languages with derived inflectional forms," they refer to the languages of the Italian-type. Both types of language allow null subjects. In contrast, since English has a type of mixed inflectional forms, null subjects are not permitted in that language. Given the well-known cross-linguistic facts, this statement is true, at most, descriptively, but one may still ask why that is so. In its essence, Jaeggli and Safir (1989) is a restatement of the facts, rather than an explanation. They themselves recognize the problem as seen in their note 20:

> "Unfortunately we do not have any answer to the natural question that arises; we have no explanation to offer as to why (26) (cited as (30) above – X.J.) should be a property of natural languages"

If what has been suggested above in this chapter is right, we can, tentatively, answer their question by saying that languages with un-derived inflectional forms permit null subjects because their I assigns Nominative Case optionally, while languages with derived inflectional forms do so because their I contains a pronominal element that, like a clitic, may discharge the obligatory assignment of Nominative Case in the place a lexical NP. In other words, by postulating an I-Parameter, which is needed independently of the null subjects issue, we have derived the language effects that have been captured under the Null Subject Parameter, at least for the cases in the Chinese-type languages.

4.4 A Generalized Case Filter (GCF)

Notice that our proposal of two sources for null subjects is crucially dependent on an assumption that Nominative Case assignment may be either obligatory or optional. It will be interesting to see whether these two options exist across different types of Case assignment generally or just for Nominative Case.

In its standard version, the Case Filter (Rouveret and Vergnaud (1980), Chomsky (1981), among many others), as given in (31) below, requires all NPs that are phonologically realized to be properly Case-marked.

(31) *NP if lexical and no Case.

The Case filter in this form is obviously a condition on Case assignees, i.e. the NPs, but says nothing about the Case assigners, i.e. those grammatical categories that perform the assignment. But given that the theory of abstract Cases, in essence, specifies a set of co-relationships between NPs and certain lexical or functional grammatical categories that are licensing the NPs in certain positions, such as the relationship between a subject NP and I̲, or between an object NP and a transitive verb, it is conceptually reasonable to assume that Case theory constrains the Case assigners in addition to the Case assignees. Put differently, under a proper reformulation of Case theory, not only does a Case assignee need a Case assigner, but also vice versa. A Case assigner, if obligatory, not only can assign a Case, but also must do so, requiring appropriate discharge. In brief, we propose a Generalized Case Filter (GCF) as in (32) below.[2]

(32) The Generalized Case Filter (GCF)

    i. *NP if lexical and no Case; and
    ii. *Obligatory Case assigner if un-discharged.

If the Case filter in its traditional formulation (as in (31)) defines a kind of unidirectional dependency between Case assignees and assigners, like that between, say, fish and water (fish need water to survive but not vice versa), then the Generalized Case Filter can be understood as specifying a relationship of bi-directional, mutual dependency like that between employers and employees, who depend on each other to survive. This conception of the Case filter, we argue, is not only conceptually reasonable, but can also subsume a number of apparently independent phenomena in interesting ways, capturing a wide range of language facts that must be captured in an appropriate theory of grammar.

It should first be noted that Case assigners, under this proposal, will be classified into two categories: obligatory and optional Case assigners. We assume that UG, in principle, allows both of these two options. How they are represented in each particular grammar may be subject to parameterizations, and also, perhaps, to lexical and morphological properties of each particular grammar. The primary purpose here is to suggest a line of research and so we assume the following distinction between optional and obligatory Case assigners as a rough sketch, leaving the details to be worked out in future work.

Optional	Obligatory
Genitive Case	Accusative Case by Prepositions
Nominative Case by $\underline{Ic}$	Nominative Case by $\underline{Ie}$
Accusative Case by verbs in some languages	Accusative Case by verbs in some languages

Recall that the sources for Case-assignments are very heterogeneous. NPs, for example, can be Case-assigned inherently or structurally. A Case assignment is obtained through head-complement government in some cases (e.g. Accusative Case) and through a head-Spec relationship in others (e.g. the Nominative and Genitive Cases). Similar to the sources for Case-assignment, the sources for Case-discharge of obligatory assignments are also heterogeneous. The obligatory assignment of Nominative Case by $\underline{Ie}$, for instance, is normally discharged by an NP. It can also be discharged by a quite diverse range of categories that includes a CP, a pronominal element contained in Italian $\underline{I}$, and perhaps a clitic. It has been noted that the relationship of a pronominal element in $\underline{I}$ to the subject NP seems quite similar to that of the clitic to the object NP (Chomsky (1981), Rizzi (1982), and Burzio (1986)). Now this point can be made precise by stating that clitics, or incorporated pronouns, are analogous to the pronominal element of $\underline{I}$ in terms of their relations to object and subject NPs respectively because they both may discharge a Case assignment to a position that is normally taken by an NP. Furthermore, a clitic may not only discharge the assignment of Accusative Case, but also may discharge an assignment of Nominative Case in languages like Italian and Pashto, which have "subject clitics." In brief, NPs, CPs, pronominal elements of $\underline{I}$ (pe = pronominal element of I in (33c)), and clitics pattern together in discharging obligatory assignments of Case in contrast with a plain empty category, which does not (as in (33e)).

(33) a. [$_{NP}$ The space shuttle] is amazing.

    b. [$_{CP}$ That space shuttles fly so high] is amazing.

    c. [$_{pe}$] ved-e Maria. (Italian)
        sees Maria
        "He sees Maria."

    d. [$_{CLITIC}$ si] e stati invitati. (Italian)
        has been invited

    e. *[e] is amazing.

Preposition stranding is not allowed in many languages. Now with the Generalized Case Filter, this fact can be seen as naturally following from a simple assumption that prepositions are always obligatory (Accusative) Case assigners. Whatever prevents prepositions from being stranded can be subsumed under the GCF. Also consider the following paradigm.

(34) a. For me to live in the campus dorm would be fun.

    b. *Me to live in the campus dorm would be fun.

    c. *For to live in the campus dorm would be fun.

Among the sentences in (34), only sentence (34a) is well-formed. It is generally assumed that sentence (34b), but not (34c), is ruled by the traditional Case filter since *me* as subject of an un-tensed clause occurs in a Caseless position. With the generalization of Case filter (GCF), both (34b) and (34c) are in violation of the Case filter so that they are both accounted for directly without additional stipulations. Sentence (34b) is ruled out because it contains a Caseless NP, whereas (34c) is ungrammatical because it has an obligatory Case assignment that is not discharged.

We assume that transitive verbs also assign Accusative Case obligatorily. This is particularly clear in the following discourse (due to Huang (1984a/b)). Although the reference of an otherwise omitted pronoun is perfectly clear, omission is still prohibited, and this restriction seems to have nothing to do with semantic or pragmatic factors:

(35) Speaker A: Did John see Bill yesterday?

Speaker B: a. Yes, he saw him.

b. *Yes, he saw [e].

CPs, pronominal elements of I̲, and clitics may function to discharge the Accusative assignment as well as Nominative assignment. A reasonable problem arising at this point is that certain languages with poor inflectional morphology like Chinese appear allow empty objects. More interestingly, in Chinese, Japanese, and Korean, there seems to be a puzzling correlation between null subjects and null objects, which appears to suggest that in those languages the Accusative assignment by verbs, like the Nominative assignment by Ic, is optional. Following Huang (1984a/b), we would like to propose that null objects are not pro, rather, they are variables bound to an NP in a "topic" position (i.e. in a higher "subject position," in our terms). The NPs originating in the object position move first to the "topic" position and then get deleted from there after movement. If this is right, then null objects are in fact equivalent to null subjects. So, we can generalize by saying that Accusative Case assignment is obligatory universally.

It is also interesting to note that the conditions on Case assignment don't necessarily hold on Case discharge. It is observed, for example, that verbs' assignment of Accusative Case is subject to a condition of "adjacency," at least in certain languages. In these languages, the verb as an assigner must be linearly adjacent to the NP that receives the assignment. Sentence (36) below, in violation of this condition, is ungrammatical. In a comparable configuration, CP's discharge of Accusative Case does not seem to obey the same condition, since (37) is a good sentence.

(36) *I like **very much** apples.
(Compare: "I like apples **very much**.")

(37) He says **confidently** that he can do the job.

4.5 "Lexical I̱"?

We have been arguing that I̱, as a functional head in the Chinese-type languages, is fundamentally different from I̱ in the English-type languages. This difference can be parameterized within the framework of the Principles and Parameters theory, and a set of cross-linguistic contrasts can be derived as a result of setting of the parameter. In the literature, this clearly is not the first attempt to parameterize I̱. Among others, Huang (1982, 1984b) and his followers (e.g. Cole et al. (1990)) claim that the I̱ in languages like Chinese is different from that in languages like English in that the former is **lexical** while the latter is **functional**. They also argue that a number of properties are observed in what they call "lexical-INFL languages," but not in "functional-INFL languages," and those properties of lexical INFL languages may arguably receive a unitary explanation on Huang's assumption. This explanation includes the four properties in (38).

(38) a. Absence of that-trace effects;
b. Long-distance reflexives;
c. "Non-gap topics;" and
d. "Topic Chains" ("Null Topics").

Huang's proposal, as we see it, represents a form of parameterization of I̱. Although Huang himself is not using the term explicitly, it is obviously translatable into a format of parameterization, especially when we ask why languages should differ in the ways Huang's proposal predicts. In fact, Huang's proposal is comparable to the one articulated here, in the sense that both assume that there are two types of I̱, and that languages will systematically differ due to this crucial difference in the nature of I̱. Our parameterization, however, differs sharply from Huang's both conceptually and empirically. Here we briefly compare Huang's proposal and ours. Then we argue that Huang's proposal is conceptually problematic, and that its desirable effects can be recast and derived more naturally.

It should first be noted that there is no conceptual ground for a claim that the Chinese I̱ is lexical in contrast with the English functional one, given the standard assumptions about the distinction between functional and lexical categories (e.g. Fukui and Speas (1985), Chomsky and Lasnik (1993)). Generally speaking, items of the lexicon are of two general types: lexical and functional. As definitional characteristics, lexical categories such as N, V, A, and P have substantive content, but functional categories such as I, C, and probably D (determiner) under the DP hypothesis, don't. Both functional and lexical categories have feature structure, but lexical categories enter into Theta-marking. The conceptual problem with Huang's assumption is that there is simply no evidence justifying that I in languages like Chinese and Japanese has substantive content, or that it enters into Theta-marking. Its counterparts in languages like English and French do not. In contrast, our assumption about the distinctive I's is based on the *prima facie* language facts. Furthermore, our proposal is supported quite strongly by language evidence, such as variation in the pattern of complements by different I's. So we can say that the "lexical I" claim is entirely stipulative and that it would be preferable to deduce the resulting desirable empirical effects, particularly those in (38) above, as a theorem following from more general principles, as we will do now.

First of all, the following sentences in (39) below, for Huang (1982) and Cole et al. (1990), illustrates the contrast between Chinese and English with respect to the so-called "that-trace effects."

(39) a. That-trace effects in English
       *Who do you think [t that left]?
    b. Absence of that-trace effects in Chinese
       [Ni zhidao [shei maile shenme]]?
       you know who bought what
    c. LF structure in Chinese
       [Shei$_i$ [ni zhidao [shenme$_j$ [t$_i$ maile t$_j$]]]]

Huang and Cole et al. assume that the Chinese sentence in (39b) is well-formed because the language's lexical I, on the assumption that the ECP can be satisfied by either lexical or antecedent government, can properly govern the subject of its clause. Since it is functional, the English I can't properly govern the subject trace, yielding an ECP violation in (39a).

However, as argued quite convincingly in the work of Aoun, Hornstein, Lightfoot, and Weinberg (1987) and Lightfoot (1991), within the generalized Binding framework, the fact that (39b) from Chinese is grammatical is simply because neither *shei* "who" nor *shenme* "what," due to the lack of Agr in Chinese I, has an accessible SUBJECT or a binding Domain. The head-government requirement as a PF condition is vacuous here since the movement takes place at LF. In other words, the issue is a matter of whether an I contains Agr in some language rather than whether the I is lexical or functional in the language.

Second, Cole et al. (1990) (but not Huang himself) argue that the lexical I assumption provides an explanation for the Chinese long-distance reflexive phenomenon, which is illustrated in (40) (a simplified form of Cole et al.'s original example. A comparable English sentence is provided in (41) for the purpose of comparison).

(40) Long-distance reflexives in Chinese.

Zhangsan$_i$ renwei [Lisi xihuan **ziji**$_i$].
*Zhangsan think Lisi like self

(41) Absence of long-distance reflexives in English

***John**$_i$ thinks [Bill likes **himself**$_i$].

With their LF movement approach, Cole et al. (1990) argue that the Chinese reflexive can move upward successive-cyclically, since VP, the only potential barrier intervening, does not have the barrierhood, being L (lexically)-marked by the lexical I (the two VP nodes in (42) below). In contrast, the English I, being functional, does not L-mark the VP, and the VP therefore constitutes a barrier, blocking the I-to-I adjunction LF movement.

(42)

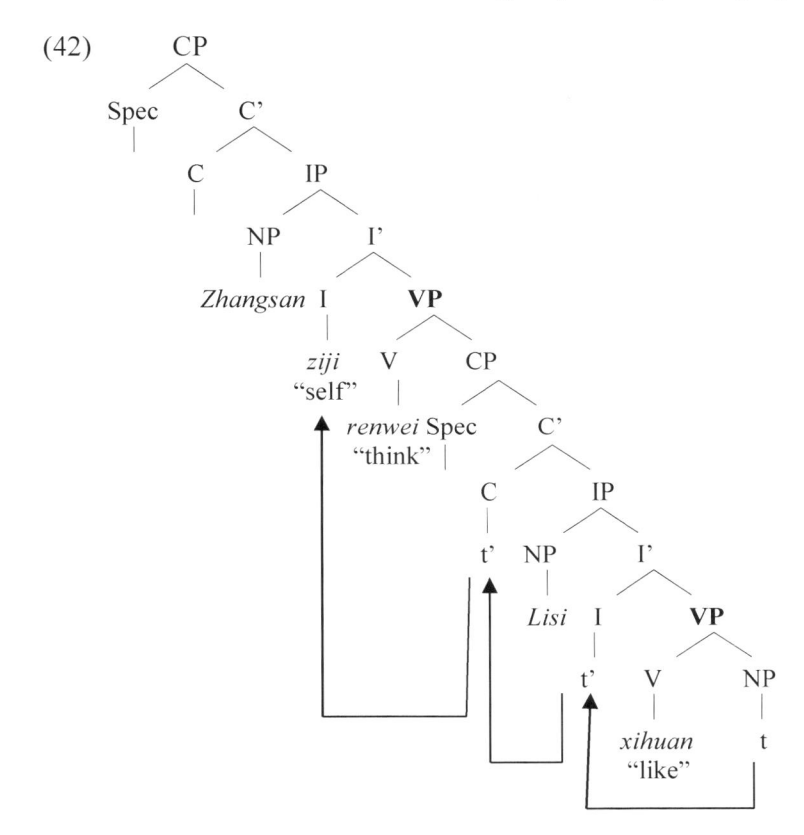

The problem with this approach, as we see it, is that it does not give a satisfactory account for contrast between the bare reflexive (i.e. *ziji* "self") and the compound reflexives (e.g. *ta-ziji* "himself") whereby only the former, but not the latter, may have long-distance antecedents. In a footnote, Cole et al. (1990) claim that compound reflexives are not long-distance anaphors because they are phrasal categories. Note that, if that is true, then their appealing to the lexical I̱ is unnecessary since English reflexives are all phrasal categories. English does not have long-distance reflexives because its reflexives are all phrasal categories. In fact, better accounts for this kind of contrast are available in the literature which do not require the lexical I̱ assumption and thus have no such problem. Huang and Tang (1988), for instance, have developed such an account. On the crucial but reasonable assumptions that anaphors must be assigned both referential and pronominal (i.e. person, number, and gender features) indices and that the assignments, if done in SS, cannot be changed in LF, Huang and Tang (1988) propose that compound reflexives with pronominal features in both Chinese and English are eligible for referential index assignment at SS, so that their reference, as provided through co-indexing with the closest local NP, is fixed at SS. Long-distance LF movement, regardless of whether it is possible, has no effect on the reference of compound reflexives in Chinese and English. On the other hand, the Chinese bare reflexive *ziji* "self," receiving only pronominal features at SS, is open to the assignment of reference indices at LF. Given the possibility of LF movement for this kind of anaphor, long-distance binding in Chinese is quite neatly derived without appealing to the lexical $\underline{I}$ assumption.

Finally, recall that the properties of "non-gap topics" (i.e. a topic NP without a corresponding co-indexed S-internal gap) and "topic chains" (i.e. properties (38c) and (38d)) were already discussed above. True, these two particular properties relate to the property of $\underline{I}$ in a given language, but not in the way that Huang and Cole et al. designate. Particularly, if a language exhibits these properties, according to our proposal, it is because it fixes the $\underline{I}$-parameter at the Chinese value so that the functional predicator $\underline{I}$ lacks the features [Tense, Agr]. The $\underline{I}$ in Chinese-type languages is not lexical either.

4.6 Summary

In this chapter we have argued that the Chinese-type $\underline{I}$ and the English-type $\underline{I}$ behave contrastively in assigning Nominative Case to the Spec position of an IP. We claim that $\underline{I}c$ assigns Nominative Case optionally in the sense that it applies only when it is needed (i.e. only when there is an NP that needs such a Case assignment), and does not require a discharge, thus allowing null subjects. In contrast, $\underline{I}e$ assigns the Nominative Case obligatorily, thus requiring an NP (which can be an expletive one) or its equivalent in the subject position, disallowing null subjects in principle. We have demonstrated that this minimal assumption provides a straightforward account for the contrast between the Chinese-type languages that permit null subjects and the English-type languages that don't. As for languages like Italian and Spanish which permit null subjects on one hand, but exhibit rich inflectional morphology (i.e. I̲e̲ languages) on the other, following Rizzi (1982) and Burzio (1986) among others, we assume that the rich I̲ in those languages contains a pronominal element, which, like a CP, a clitic, or an expletive, may function to discharge the obligatory Nominative Case assignment in the place of a lexical NP, although such an element does not require a Case-assignment. We propose that there exist two types of null subjects and consequently two types of null subject languages, and that Italian permits null subjects for fundamentally different reasons from Chinese (in this way we derive the effects of the 'Null Subject Parameter' disjunctively). According to our proposal, it is expected that the property of null subjects clusters with different sets of properties in different types of null subject languages (e.g. the free subject inversion property that is supposed to follow from the null subject property is attested only in the Italian-like null subject languages, but not in languages like Chinese). Furthermore, we suggest that the optional and obligatory assignments of Nominative Case represent only partial effects of a much more general UG principle which we formulated as the "Generalized Case Filter (GCF)." The GCF specifies a relationship of bi-directional and mutual dependency between Case assigners and assignees, so that an NP (if lexical) needs Case-assignment (by an assigner), and the assignment (if obligatory) must be properly discharged to an assignee.

We have briefly reviewed Huang's lexical I̲ proposal, arguing that functional categories are functional universally. We noted that Huang's hypothesis, given the reasonably well established distinction between lexical and functional categories (e.g. in Fukui and Speas (1985), and in Chomsky and Lasnik (1993)), has no conceptual ground, and the empirical language facts that it captures may best be derived as theorem of more general and independently motivated principles, including the I̲-Parameter.

Notes

[1] The question arising here is why Nominative Case is not assigned to the post-verbal NP to the right rather than to the null subject to the left so that i-subjects will be allowed independently of the nature of the pre-verbal null subject. Evidence from the infinitives, as Burzio (1986) argues convincingly, suggests that this is not possible. See Burzio (1986) for the illustration.

[2] We note that this assumption raises a question as to how Case assignment relates to Sub-categorization, especially if one assumes some form of the Visibility Hypothesis, which relates Case-assignment to theta-role assignment at LF. In fact, it makes the former a necessary condition for the latter to apply. To answer this question, we adopt an idea of Raposo and Uriagereka (p.c.) who, based on the fact that Case can be assigned to the non-raised subject of complement Small Clause by a matrix verb with which it has no theta-relation at all, argue that the traditional Case Filter that has its own status in the grammar must be kept.

Chapter 5

Null Object and Its Syntactic Derivation[*]

ABSTRACT: *In this chapter, an alternative explanatory framework is offered to accommodate the subject-object asymmetry phenomenon and the apparent Subjacency-violating null object constructions in Chinese. It is also argued that a topic position is always available syntactically, but an NP there could either be base-generated or moved from somewhere else. A null object in the language is a trace created by A'-movement of a pro to a topic position of its own clause, which could be a topic position of a relative clause, then from there the pro may or may not move further up if all applicable conditions, such as the Subjacency condition, allow it to do so. In those constructions that appear to have violated the Subjacency condition, the object trace, variable, is in fact not created by an A'-movement to the matrix topic position. Rather, it is a trace created by an A'-movement of pro to an embedded topic position. The lexical NP in the matrix topic position is base-generated in-situ, thus the Subjacency condition is adhered to. The co-reference between the NP in the matrix topic position and the null object in embedded clauses is made possible indirectly through two independent steps: The first step is an A'-movement of a pro from the object position to the embedded topic position within the same clause; and the second one is a co-indexing process that co-indexes the NP in the matrix topic position and the pro in the embedded topic position as an effect of Huang's Generalized Control Rule (GCR).*

---

[*]A version of this chapter originally appeared with the title "The Nature of Null Objects in Chinese" in *Journal of Chinese Language and Computing* 16:1 (2006), pp. 1–15. Revisions made are technical and minimal, the essential contents remain unchanged. It is included in this monograph as a chapter with kind permission from the Chinese and Oriental Languages Information Processing Society, Singapore.

5.1 Introduction

Works in generative grammar have devoted considerable attention to null objects in natural languages. One reason is that there generally is no overt connection between morphological agreement and the occurrence of null objects, even in languages such as Portuguese, in which such a connection can be claimed between morphological agreement and subjects. Thus, the features of null objects are likely to be reflections of innate language mechanisms. More importantly, in the highly modularized syntactic framework that this study adopts, any claim made about the status of null objects in individual languages may have theoretical implications for other components of Universal Grammar, such as the empty category (or EC) typology, Empty Category Principle (ECP), Binding Conditions, and the Subjacency Condition.

This chapter will start with some remarks on what has been termed subject-object asymmetry in terms of the referential possibility of the null categories, focusing especially on some criticisms some authors have put forward against Huang's original proposal (Section 5.2). Section 5.3 will be devoted to a discussion of superficial Subjacency condition violations observed in null object constructions under the hypothesis that null objects are movement-created variables. As will be demonstrated, it is largely due to dependence on the functional determination of empty categories that the issue is left unsolved in Huang (1984), thus it is often taken as an important argument against the null-object-as-variable proposal. Additionally, Cole (1987), with his two diagnostic tools for the treatment of null objects, will be shown to have created a dilemma in categorizing Chinese null objects since the language exhibits subject-object asymmetry on one hand, and it allows Subjacency condition violations on the other. An alternate proposal will be presented in Section 5.4, which is a set of extensions and modifications of Ni and Huang's ideas. The conclusions of this study and a number of assumptions necessary to reach them will be summarized in Section 5.5.

5.2 The Subject-Object Asymmetry

As Huang (1984, 1987) has observed, in languages like Chinese, Japanese and Korean, there are some restrictions on the reference of an empty category if it occurs as an object, but not if it is used a subject. That is, in the most natural context in which pragmatic or discourse factors are reduced to the minimum, the empty category in an embedded subject position is free in reference: It may refer to the matrix subject or to some other entity whose reference is distinct from the subject, whereas an empty category in an embedded object position may only take as its antecedent an NP whose reference is fixed outside of the entire sentence, but not the matrix subject (crucially, it cannot simply can co-refer with that NP). Some of Huang's original examples are as follows.

(1) a. Zhangsan$_i$ shuo [e$_i$ bu renshi Lisi]
    Zhangsan say   not know Lisi
    "Zhangsan said that (he) did not know Lisi."

  b. *Zhangsan$_i$ shuo [Lisi bu renshi e$_i$]
    Zhangsan say   Lisi not know
    Intended: "Zhangsan said that Lisi did not know (him)."

(2) a. Zhangsan$_i$ xiwang [e$_i$ keyi kanjian Lisi]
    Zhangsan hope   can see Lisi
    "Zhangsan hopes that (he) can see Lisi."

  b. *Zhangsan$_i$ xiwang [Lisi keyi kanjian e$_i$]
    Zhangsan hope   Lisi can see
    Intended: "Zhangsan hopes that Lisi can see (him)."

Huang's account for this asymmetry goes quite neatly as follows: The embedded subject EC may be a pronominal since it can be locally bound by the matrix subject *Zhangsan*, which has its own independent thematic role. The object EC, on the other hand, cannot be a pronominal since it cannot bound by the matrix subject. Rather, the object EC is bound by a topic NP that may or may not be phonetically realized. Obviously, this topic position is a non-argument (non-A) and non-thematic position. By the principle of functional determination of ECs, such an EC is a variable. As a variable, the EC is required by Principle C of the Binding Theory to be A-free.

Since its publication, Huang (1984) has drawn considerable attention from scholars working in the area. Some writers have extended the hypothesis, which has been established on the basis of Asian languages, to such languages as Portuguese, Spanish, and Kinande, obtaining a much wider range of empirical support (e.g. Hasegawa (1985), Raposo (1986), and Campos (1986), among others). Meanwhile, this hypothesis has also given rise to some controversies that are unsurprising within such an intricate theoretical system. For example, Cole (1987) argued that the overall treatment of object ECs in languages around the world should be parameterized, and that Huang's generalization of object EC as a variable may be right for some languages, but not for other languages, such as Imbabura. Some other writers have challenged the hypothesis either empirically or conceptually (e.g. Xu (1986) and Ni (1987), among others).

Xu's (1986) challenge is largely a factual dispute about the existence of subject-object asymmetry. He provides some examples to show that the asymmetry does not exist in Chinese. While this kind of dispute may continue, we assume with Huang that the asymmetry does hold at least for many native speakers, if not for all, in contexts where pragmatic or discourse considerations are reduced to a minimum. In my opinion, Xu's (1986) contribution is his observation that there appears to be a set of Chinese sentences with object ECs in which the Subjacency condition seems to be violated. The question, to which Huang's response is not satisfactory, will be addressed in next section.

Ni (1987) is remarkable. The article is meant to reconcile the two extreme positions of Huang and Xu, but it ends up being a real challenge to Huang (1984). The most interesting observation presented in Ni's article is that an embedded clause may have a topic as well as a matrix sentence. As Ni himself claims, a topic is allowed in every clause, just as it is allowed in every sentence. Being perfectly consistent with native speakers' intuition and supported by further empirical language data, such a proposal will be explored and modified as a possible solution to the problematic issues concerning Subjacency condition violations in Section 4 of this paper. However, we will demonstrate that the proposal in Ni's original formulation will run into serious difficulty as he attempts to reach a unified account for both null subjects and objects in Chinese and do away with the subject-object asymmetry.

Ni's argument is as follows: Given that every clause may theoretically have a topic overtly or covertly, nothing, in principle, prohibits each sentence in (1a) and (1b) from having an embedded null topic (henceforth, ET) that both the null subject and the null object may take as their antecedents. In other words, sentences (1a) and (1b) could be analyzed as (3) and (4) respectively in a technical sense at some level of representation.

(3) Zhangsan shuo [ET_i [e_i bu renshi Lisi]]
   Zhangsan say   not know Lisi
   "Zhangsan said that (ET) (he) did not know Lisi."

(4) Zhangsan shuo [ET_i [Lisi bu renshi e_i]]
   Zhangsan say   Lisi not know
   "Zhangsan said that (ET) Lisi did not know (him)."

If the above analysis is correct, as Ni argues, the subject EC in (3) and the object EC in (4) are both locally A'-bound by an embedded topic in the same sense; hence, they are both variables under Chomsky's (1981) empty category typology. A unified account for subject and object ECs is thus achieved.

What is especially problematic about this proposal is its identification of the status of embedded topics. Although Ni may be right to say that every clause may theoretically have a topic in a general sense, he does not make it clear that the occurrence of such ECs, in particular syntactic configurations, is also constrained by relevant principles. The Binding conditions, as illustrated by the contrast among the following examples, are among the applicable principles at work.

(5) Wangwu shuo Zhangsan$_i$ Lisi kanjian-le e$_i$.
    Wangwu say Zhangsan Lisi see-Asp
    "Wangwu said that, Zhangsan, Lisi had seen (him)."

(6) *Ta$_i$ shuo Zhangsan$_i$ Lisi kanjian-le e$_i$.
    he say Zhangsan Lisi see-Asp
    Intended "He said that, Zhangsan, Lisi had seen (him)."

(7) *Zhangsan$_i$ shuo ta$_i$ Lisi kanjian-le e$_i$.
    Zhangsan say he Lisi see-Asp
    Intended Meaning"Zhangsan said that, him, Lisi had seen (him)."

Note that the above ungrammatical sentences (6) and (7) are in no violation of any known principles except that the topic NPs of the embedded clauses, i.e. *Zhangsan* in (6) and *ta* "him" in (7), are A-bound by the matrix subject NPs *ta* "he" and *Zhangsan* respectively. This phenomenon can be accounted for only if we assume that NPs in A'-positions are subject to the Binding principles just as those in A-positions. Assuming that each topic NP occupies a specifier position of a CP, and from there the NP is governed by a matrix verb, we note that the binding domain for an embedded topic can only be the matrix sentence. Thus, (6) is ungrammatical because its embedded topic, *Zhangsan*, is an R-expression that violates Principle C of the Binding theory, while (7) violates Principle B since the embedded topic *ta* "he" is co-referential with the matrix subject NP *Zhangsan*.

If the above analysis is correct, then the hypothesis that sentences like (3) have an embedded null topic cannot be right, regardless of whether the null category is a pronominal (pro) or a nominal (variable) since the sentences with such a category would have violated the very same principles that sentences (6) and (7) do. On the other hand, given that (3) is a perfectly acceptable sentence, the proposal made by Ni must be wrong.

Furthermore, based on the assumption that the embedded empty topic is pronominal (pro), the hypothesis that there exists such an ET in (4) doesn't work out either. That such an empty pronominal is impossible is not only because it is a potential violation of Principle B, but also because it is a violation of the Generalized Control Rule (GCR) (Huang (1985)). GCR requires a pronominal empty category to be co-indexed with the closest possible antecedent, which, in this case, is the subject NP *Zhangsan*. Contrary to the prediction of the hypothesis, *Zhangsan* can't be co-referential with the ET, if it exists in the first place. We will return to this issue in Section 4 below.

However, one may still argue that empty categories may behave differently from overt lexical categories. Although empty categories don't have to behave like their corresponding overt lexical counterparts in every way, and could differ in many aspects, they do have to behave alike in terms of Binding conditions since that is essentially the very feature that makes them pattern together.

5.3 The Subjacency Condition

In an interesting attempt to parameterize languages by null object properties, Cole (1987) demonstrates that the following four types of languages exist, based on their treatment of null objects.

Language Types	Null Pronominal Object	Null Variable Object
I	−	+
II	+	−
III	+	+
IV	−	−

Cole argues that there are two parameters at work that give rise to the full range of null object possibilities in languages.

Parameter 1: Infl Government Parameter (IGP)
Languages differ in whether they have lexical Infl as a proper governor. If a language has lexical Infl as a proper governor, then theoretically it is

possible for it to have a base-generated null topic, since it may be governed by the lexical Infl. One of the consequences of this is that the language may have variable objects. This parameter distinguishes languages like English and Imbabura, in which Infl is not a proper governor, from languages in which it is, such as Chinese, Portuguese, Korean, and Thai. The IGP predicts that the first group of languages will not allow variable null objects, and the second group of languages will.

Parameter 2: Generalized Control Rule Parameter (GCRP)

Languages contrast with respect to whether the GCR (Huang (1985)) applies to both pro and PRO or to PRO only. This parameter determines whether null pronominal objects are allowed. Since it applies to both pro and PRO in Chinese, Portuguese, and English, these languages don't allow null pronominal objects. As it applies only to PRO in Imbabura, Korean, and Thai, these languages are theoretically allowed to have null pronominal objects.

Taken together, the relationship between these two parameters and the nature of the null objects in natural languages can be schematized in the following table.

Language Types	Generalized Control Rule Parameter (GCRP)	Infl Government Parameter (IGP)
	Null Pronominal Object	Null Variable Object
I: Chinese; Portuguese	−	+
II: Imbabura	+	−
III: Korean, and Thai	+	+
IV: English	−	−

Generally speaking, these two neatly formulated parameters give us the correct predictions, as Cole demonstrates in his article. According to this proposal, it is predicted that Chinese and Portuguese will allow null variable objects, but not null pronominal objects. The diagnostic tools by which he justifies his claim about the status of null objects in a particular language are the following:

[1] Subject-object asymmetry in the distribution of empty categories

That is, an empty category in an embedded subject position can be co-referential with the subject, but an empty category in an embedded object position cannot be. This is attested in both Chinese and Portuguese. The relevant Chinese data has already been discussed above in sentences (1) and (2). The following pair of sentences is from Portuguese, which clearly demonstrates such a subject-object asymmetry.

(8) a.   Empty subject
          Ele$_i$ pensa [que e$_i$ perguntou-me].
          he   thinks that   asked me
          "He thinks that (he) asked me."

    b.   Empty object
          *Ele$_i$ pensa [que eu recomendei e$_i$ ao professor]
          he   thinks that I recommended   to professor
          Intended Meaning: "He thinks that I recommended (him) to the professor."

[2] The distribution of empty objects is sensitive to the Subjacency condition.

This is to say that empty objects may not occur in complex NPs or in sentential subject NPs. This is an expected result if the empty object undergoes a movement that crosses two bounding nodes, violating the Subjacency condition. It is not expected if the empty category is a pro, which is presumably base-generated in its surface position, rather than moved. This prediction is also attested in Portuguese (Raposo (1986)).

(9) a. Simple clause

O rapaz trouxe e mesmo agora da pastelaria
the boy brought same   now of the-bakery
"The boy brought (something) right now from the
bakery."

b. Relative clause

*O rapaz que trouxe *e* mesmo agora da pastelaria era o
the boy   that brought   same now   of the-bakery was the
teu afilhado
your godson
Intended Meaning: "The boy that brought (something)
right now from the bakery was your godson."

What is most interesting here is that the same prediction is not attested in Chinese. In fact, the distribution of empty objects in the language appears not to be constrained by the Subjacency condition. As one of the major arguments against Huang's null-object-as-variable proposal, Xu (1986) and Ni (1987) provide many examples to demonstrate that the relationship between a topic and a sentence-internal gap is not subject to island conditions. Several types of sentences from Chinese are in apparent violation of the Subjacency condition. Some examples are:

(10) Zhe ben shu$_i$ [$_{NP}$ [$_S$ EC du-guo EC$_i$ de] ren] bu duo.
this CL book   read-Asp   man not many
"This book, the people (who) have read (it) are not many."

(11) Zhe xie shi$_i$ [$_{NP}$ [$_S$ ta shuo EC$_i$]] bu heshi.
these CL things   he say   not appropriate
"These things, that he says are not appropriate."

As pointed out by Xu (1986), the null object in (10) is separated from the topic position of the whole sentence by an NP node and an S node, and the latter is a relative clause. The null object in (11) is located in a sentential subject position, which is a typical island. In both sentences, the topic NPs and the null objects are separated by at least two bounding nodes. Thus, the grammatical sentences (10) and (11) constitute counter examples to the Subjacency condition, given that that null objects are variables created by A'-movement. This observation, among others, leads to Xu's and Ni's conclusion that topic constructions in Chinese don't involve movement, and that those empty categories in the object position are not traces (variables) generated by A'-movement.

If he takes the above fact into consideration, Cole's theory leaves a paradox created partially by his own null object identification diagnostic tools. Note that Chinese, on one hand, exhibits subject-object asymmetry, so its null objects must be variables; on the other hand, the same language appears to not obey the Subjacency condition in null object constructions, although the same locality condition is observed in many other constructions in the language. This suggests that null objects in Chinese cannot be variables, and are, perhaps, null pronominals (i.e. pro).

Huang's (1984) solution to this problem is not satisfactory either, since the solution is very much contingent upon the Functional Determination Theory of empty categories, which has to allow ECs to change their status in the course of a syntactic derivation. Huang claims that an empty category like that in an object position may start out as a pronominal one at the D-Structure, and later be co-indexed with an NP in a topic position, thus becoming a variable at the S-Structure. According to Huang's functional definition of empty categories, it is a variable just because it is co-indexed with an NP in an A' (topic) position. Those empty categories in the object position are not derived by movement, thus the Subjacency condition is not applicable here. Note that this proposal is based on a crucial assumption that the identity of an empty category may change in the course of a derivation. However, this hypothesis, as Huang (1987) himself notices later, is likely to be wrong. As Epstein (1983/1984), among others, argues convincingly, an empty category may not change its status of identity in the course of a syntactic derivation, thus the functional definition of ECs cannot deal with the problems we raise here. If an empty category is a variable, it has to be created by movement under the constraint of the Subjacency condition and all other applicable principles.

Given these discussions, it makes good sense for us to seek an optimal account that not only accommodates the subject-object asymmetry phenomenon and the apparent Subjacency condition violations, but also is independent from the functional theory of empty categories. As we proceed with this discussion in the next section, we will see that such a solution is possible.

5.4 Null Object in Chinese in Its Derivation

In this section, we shall argue that null objects in Chinese can only be variables, and that the Subjacency condition is observed in the language on the other.

We assume that every clause, including relative and normal clauses, has a topic position, and that regardless of whether it is filled by a lexical NP or left empty, the position, as a syntactic slot, is always there. We argue that the Subjacency condition is observed even in the sentences discussed above, which appear to have violated the condition since the null pronominal (pro) may move to an embedded topic position, the null pronominal remains in the embedded topic position, and from there it binds to a variable in an object position in the same clause. Additionally, there is a process of co-indexing that will eventually give rise to the co-reference between the null pronominal in the embedded topic position and the NP in the topic position of the matrix sentence. Unlike Huang's, this new account is independent of the Functional Determination Theory of ECs. Instead, we adopt Epstein's proposal by which ECs can only be identified by derivation and the identity of a given EC cannot change in the course of a derivation.

Let us begin our derivation by asking a very basic question that any theory intending to deal with null objects has to confront: How are NPs in topic positions derived in a language? Is it base-generated *in situ* or moved there from somewhere else?

Given that the Chinese language exhibits the subject-object asymmetry phenomenon, and that some topic NPs don't have sentence-internal gaps in the language, it is reasonable to assume that a Chinese topic NP is base-generated in some sentences, but has been moved there from some other position in others. The following criteria serve to make a distinction between the two.

If a topic NP does not have a sentence-internal gap to be co-referential with, then it must be base-generated there. This is the so-called "non-gap topic" (Cole (1987)).

(12) Shuiguo, wo xihuan pingguo.
     fruit   I   like   apple
     "As for fruits, I like apples."

(13) Nei chang huo, xingkui xiaofangdui lai-de zao.
     that CL fire fortunately fire-brigade come early
     "As for that fire, fortunately the fire brigade came early."

If a topic NP is co-referential with a sentence-internal gap or has a trace that is co-referential with a sentence-internal gap, then it must have been moved there from some other position.

(14) Nei bu shu$_i$, wo du-le EC$_i$.
     that CL book I read-Asp
     "That book, I have read (it)."

(15) Wangwu$_i$, Zhangsan shuo t$_i$ Lisi renshi EC$_i$.
     Wangwu Zhangsan say   Lisi know
     "Wangwu, Zhangsan said that Lisi knows (him)."

The topic NPs in sentences (14) and (15) above have been moved there, since they either are co-referential with a sentence-internal gap as in (14), or have a trace that is co-referential with a sentence-internal gap as in (16). Assuming that a topic position takes the specifier position of a CP, we can say that the D-Structure and derivation of a sentence like (15) should be something like that in (16) below.

(16)

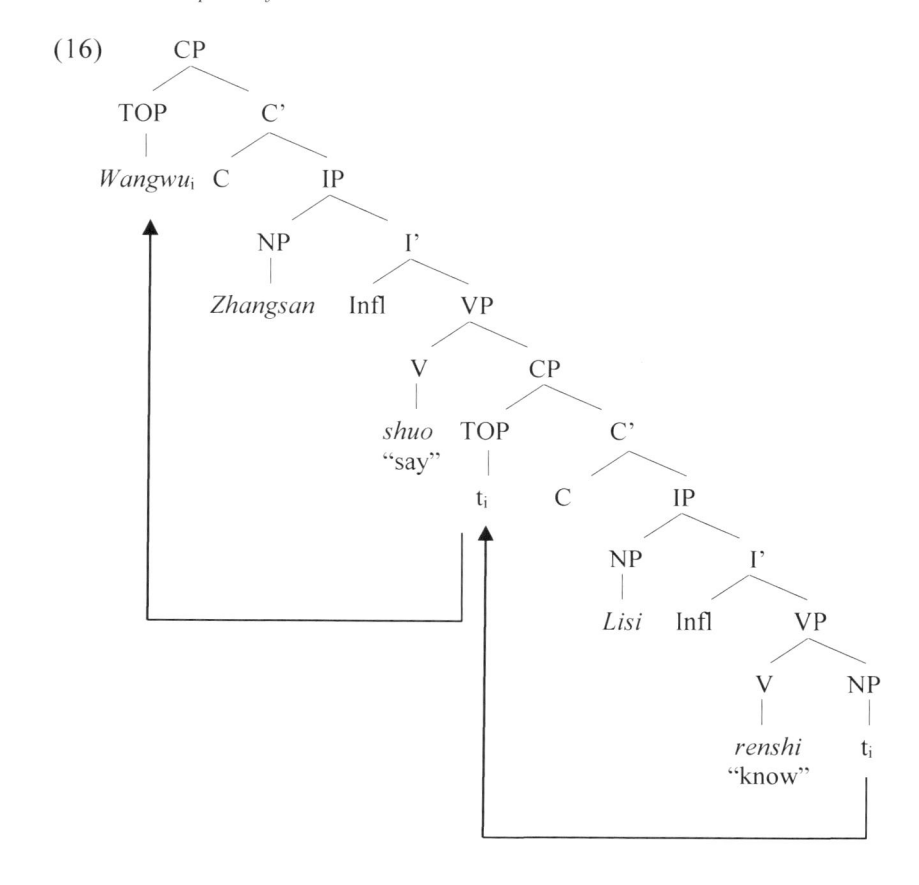

We now may turn to the Subjacency condition issue, which we refer as Cole's paradox. Based on Ni's approach concerning embedded topics, I would take a further step and claim that it is not only a regular clause that can have a topic position, even a relative clause within an NP may also have a topic position. To account for the apparent Subjacency-violating facts, we would argue that, although null objects are variables generated by A'-movement to topic positions, nothing, crucially, in principle requires them to move to the topic positions of matrix sentences in violation of the Subjacency condition. Rather, it is perfectly possible for them to just move to an embedded topic position (e.g. a topic position of a relative clause or that of a sentential subject clause) and simply remain there. On the previous assumption that the out-moving constituent is a pronominal empty category (pro), the null pronominal in an embedded topic position can simply be co-indexed with an NP in the matrix topic position through an independently defined co-indexing process. Thus, the D-Structure and derivational course of sentence (10), repeated below as (17), could be illustrated as in (18).

(17)   Zhe ben shu$_i$ [$_{NP}$ [$_S$ EC du-guo EC$_i$ de] ren] bu duo.
　　　this CL book　　　　　read-Asp　　people not many
　　　"This book, the people (who) have read (it) are not many."

(18)

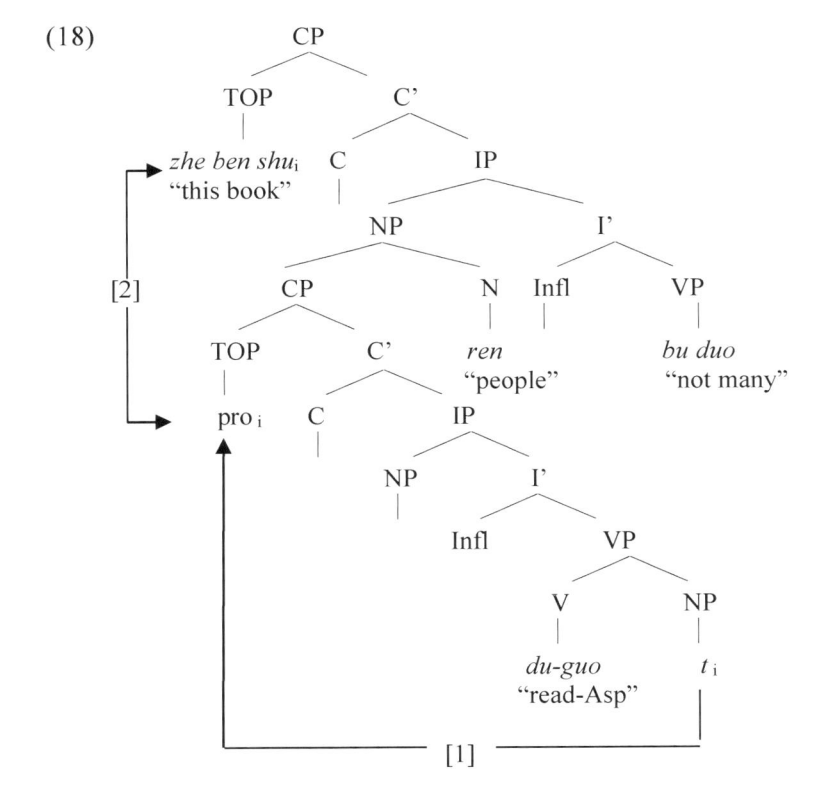

This analysis deserves some further clarification and emphasis.

First of all, please note that the NP in the matrix topic position *zhe ben shu* "this book" is base-generated there, but the null object of verb *du-guo* "read" is a variable created by an A'-movement. At first, there may seem to be a contradiction between these two statements; however, recall that an NP in a topic position could be either base-generated or movement-created, depending on whether it has a co-referential sentence-internal gap or a trace which, in turn, has a co-referential sentence-internal gap. By this definition, we can say the NP in the matrix topic position is base-generated there, since it has neither. The null object, although co-referential with the NP *zhe ben shu* "this book" in the matrix topic position, does not have to be a trace/variable created by an NP-movement to the matrix topic position. Rather, it is created by the movement of an empty pronominal category (pro) to the embedded topic position (i.e. Movement Step [1] in (18)) above). The co-reference between the matrix topic NP and the null object is derived indirectly: By the trace theory of movement, the trace in the object position is co-indexed with its antecedent "pro" in the embedded topic position automatically; then such a "pro," in turn, is co-indexed with the matrix topic NP by an independent process, possibly as an effect of Huang's (1985) Generalized Control Rule (i.e. Step [2] in (18)).

Secondly, note that this apparent Subjacency-violating sentence involves a relative clause. As widely assumed in the literature, where no embedded topic position of relative clauses is recognized, the relativization process in Chinese generally involves the movement of an empty operator to a COMP position, and from there it is co-indexed with the head noun (e.g. *ren* "people" in (18)). According to our proposal, there is an embedded topic position that appears to intervene between the empty operator and the head noun, blocking the co-indexation process between the two nominal categories. Tackling this problematic issue, we, in the spirit of Cole and Sung's (1990) "Feature Percolation Principles",[1] assume that the referential index of the empty operator in the head category of the CP percolates up to its dominating node (i.e. CP) along with all its other features. Then, the co-indexing takes place as usual under the condition concerned, as if the TOP position is not filled.

As for the sentential subject NP island, we propose that the D-Structure and derivation of sentence (11), repeated below as (19), could be illustrated as in (20).

(19) Zhe xie shi$_i$ [$_{NP}$ [$_S$ ta shuo EC$_i$]] bu heshi.
　　these CL things　　he say　　　not appropriate
　　"These things, that he says is not appropriate."

(20)

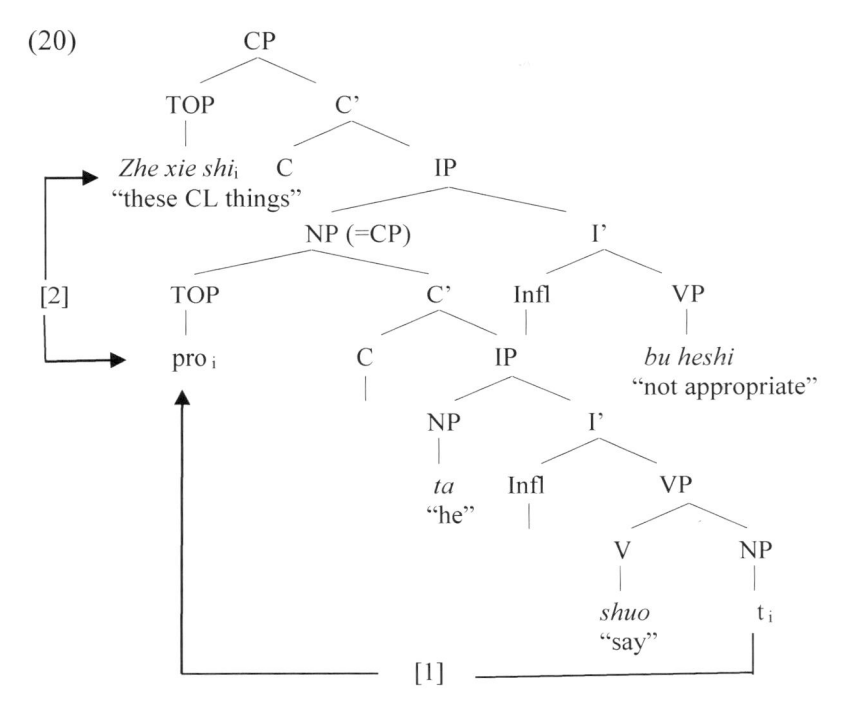

Very much like its counterpart in (18), the NP *zhe xie shi* "these things" in the matrix topic position can also be considered to be base-generated. The null object, although co-referential with the matrix topic NP, is also a variable created by the movement of a pro to the embedded topic position (i.e. Step [1] in (20) above), rather than by a direct movement to the matrix topic position, since the latter will be forced to cross at least two bounding nodes and be in violation of the Subjacency condition. Once again, we assume that the antecedent of the null object variable is a pro. And by the GCR, it got co-indexed with the matrix topic NP automatically, since it is the closest NP accessible to the pro (i.e. Step [2] in (20)). Crucially, the subject position (the one taken by *ta* "he") of the embedded clause, which is structurally lower than the topic position of the clause, is correctly predicted not to be the antecedent of the pro. Note that this analysis also constitutes an additional argument for our null-object-as-variable approach and against the null-object-as-pro approach (Li (1985), among others). According to the null-object-as-pro approach, a null object is base-generated as a pro in the post-verbal object position and will remain there throughout the whole course of a derivation. By the GCR, a pro, as well as a PRO, has to be co-indexed with the closest NP. If so, then the NP in the embedded subject position will be wrongly predicted to be co-referential with the null object in a direct violation of Principle B.

As has been pointed out in Section 5.2 above, an embedded null topic NP, contrary to what Ni claims, is impossible in a sentence containing a null subject as illustrated in (3) (repeated below as (21)), since the empty topic, regardless of whether it is a pronominal or nominal/R-expression, will be in violation of one of the binding principles. Now, if the embedded empty topic is a pro, as argued above, then it also will be ruled out by the GCR (not by Principle B) in a sentence containing a null object, as in (4) (repeated as (22)).

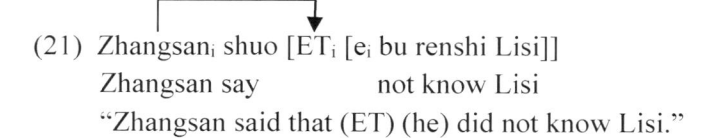

(21) Zhangsan$_i$ shuo [ET$_i$ [e$_i$ bu renshi Lisi]]
      Zhangsan say   not know Lisi
      "Zhangsan said that (ET) (he) did not know Lisi."

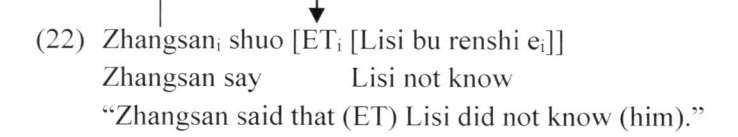

(22) Zhangsan$_i$ shuo [ET$_i$ [Lisi bu renshi e$_i$]]
      Zhangsan say   Lisi not know
      "Zhangsan said that (ET) Lisi did not know (him)."

It is impossible for the ET to remain in the embedded topic position of (22) since it will be wrongly co-indexed with the matrix subject, which is the closest potential antecedent under Huang's definition of the GCR. The correct analysis of (22), therefore, should be (22') below.

(22') pro$_i$ Zhangsan$_i$ shuo [t$_i$ [Lisi bu renshi t$_i$]]

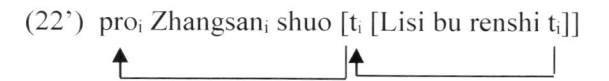

As an extra piece of confirming evidence for our proposal, our account, working together with Huang's GCR, may also give a desirable explanation of another subject-object asymmetry because "extraction" is permitted from a complex NP in a subject position, as in (23) below, but not from that in an object position, as in (24), as first pointed out in Huang (1984).

(23) Complex NP in a subject position
      Nei ben shu$_i$ [du-guo de EC$_i$ xuesheng] bu duo.
      that CL book read-Aps students   not many
      "As for that book, the students (who) have read (it) are not
      many."

(24) Complex NP in an object position
      *Nei ben shu$_i$, wo jian-guo [du-guo EC$_i$ de xuesheng].
      that CL book   I meet-Asp read-Asp   students
      Intended: "As for that book, I have met the students (who) have
      read (it)."

To account for the above asymmetry, Huang has to stipulate that the GCR applies before the identification of the EC status under the Functional Determination Theory. If Huang does not make this ad hoc stipulation, the functional determination of EC will automatically convert the null object, which is presumably a pro at D-Structure in both sentences above, into variables since they are each bound by an NP in an A' topic position. This renders the GCR irrelevant, since the GCR is essentially a referential condition on pro and PRO only, not on variables. In other words, Huang has to make an extra stipulation in order to account for the subject-object asymmetry exhibited in (23) and (24).

An account under our above proposal is much simpler and much more natural than Huang's. As proposed above, the NPs in the matrix topic position in both (23) and (24) are base-generated, and the null objects in both sentences are variables created by a movement of a pro to an A' embedded topic position. In other words, the sentences in (23) and (24) can be analyzed as (23') and (24'), respectively, at the level of S-Structure where the GCR applies.

(23') Nei ben shu$_i$ [[[pro$_i$ [e du-guo de t$_i$]] xuesheng] bu duo.
      that CL book   read-Aps   students   not many
      "As for that book, the students (who) have read (it) are not
      many."

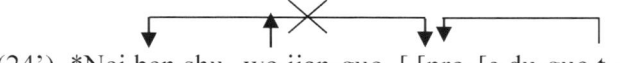

(24') *Nei ben shu$_i$, wo jian-guo [[pro$_i$ [e du-guo t$_i$ de]] xuesheng].
      that CL book   I meet-Asp   read-Asp   students
      Intended: "As for that book, I have met the students (who)
      have read (it)."

By the GCR, a pro must be identified by the closest potential antecedent. Note that the closest antecedent for the pro in (23') is the NP *nei ben shu* "that book" in the matrix topic position. The pro, after being moved to the embedded topic position from the post-verbal object position, is correctly identified as being co-referential with the matrix topic NP.[2] However, The pro in (24'), after being moved to the embedded topic position from the post-verbal object position, cannot be identified as being co-referential with the matrix topic NP since there is an NP *wo* "I" in the matrix subject position, which is even closer to the pro than the matrix topic NP, blocking the co-indexing process. Sentence (24) is ill-formed, as the theory predicts. This is exactly the language fact; thus, the asymmetry is derived naturally, without any additional stipulations.

5.5 Summary

NPs in A' topic positions are subject to the Binding conditions just as they are in A-positions. Although he is right in a general sense in claiming that every clause has a topic position, fulfilled or empty, Ni's (1987) unified account for both null subjects and null objects in Chinese is incomplete since a pro in an embedded topic position will be ruled out either by Principle B, if the embedded clause has a null subject, or by the Generalized Control Rule, if the clause has a null object. Huang's proposal of the subject-object asymmetry that null subjects are pro's, and null objects are variables still stands against Ni's challenge.

We have argued that although Huang is right in analyzing Chinese null objects as variables, he is perhaps wrong in claiming that those variables are not trace-created by A'-movement and that the variables are determined functionally (which is based on an incorrect assumption that an empty category may change its status during the course of a syntactic derivation). Although his two diagnostic tools for identifying null object typology are neatly defined, Cole (1987) eventually will find that in categorizing the Chinese language within his typological framework, he has created a dilemma: Null objects in Chinese are variables and pro's at the same time. Chinese null objects must be variables according to Cole (1987) since the language exhibits subject-object asymmetry; at the same time, those empty categories must be pro's, since apparent Subjacency-violating constructions are observed in which the null objects are separated from their respective potential antecedents (i.e. the NPs in the matrix topic positions) by two or more bounding nodes.

In this chapter, we have articulated an alternative proposal that not only accounts for the subject-object asymmetry phenomenon and the apparent Subjacency-violating null object constructions, but also is independent of the Functional Determination Theory of empty categories. We argue that in languages like Chinese, the topic position, as a syntactic slot, is always there, but an NP in the position could be either base-generated *in-situ* or moved there from somewhere else. A null object in the language is a trace (thus, a variable) created by A'-movement of a D-Structure pro to a topic position of its own clause (which could be a topic position of a relative clause), then from there, the pro may or may not move further up if all applicable conditions, such as the Subjacency condition, allow it to do so. In the constructions that appear to have violated the Subjacency condition, the object trace (variable) is, in fact, not created by an A'-movement to the matrix topic position. Rather, it is a trace created by an A'-movement of pro to an embedded topic position. The lexical NP in the matrix topic position is base-generated, and so the Subjacency condition is observed. The co-reference between the NP in the matrix topic position and the null object is derived indirectly through two independent steps: The first step is an A'-movement of a pro from the object position to the embedded topic position within the same clause; the second step is a co-indexing process that co-indexes the NP in the matrix topic position and the pro in the embedded topic position, perhaps as an effect of Huang's Generalized Control Rule (GCR).

Note finally that our proposal is based on a number of assumptions to which our study can, in turn, be interpreted as providing additional confirming supports: [1] A relative clause may have a topic position just like all other types of clauses; [2] NPs in topic positions could be either base-generated or movement-created, and [3] The movement involved in Chinese topicalization is a type of syntactic movement which, like any other syntactic movement, is working under the strict constraint of applicable locality conditions.

Notes

[1] The Feature Percolation Principles (Cole and Sung (1990)) are stated as follows:

[1] The features of all the daughters of the head node will percolate upward to the mother. Thus, the features of the mother will be a combination of the features of all daughters.

[2] In cases of feature conflict among the daughter nodes, the mother node will have the features of the head.

[3] In downward percolation, features will percolate from the mother to the head but not to other daughter nodes.

Extending this approach, we can assume that the [+Wh/-Wh] feature as well as pronominal features and referential index will percolate upward from a daughter node to its mother node. For example:

(i)   Wo xiangzhidao shei lai-le.
       I   wonder   who come-Asp
       'I wonder who has come.'

(ii)

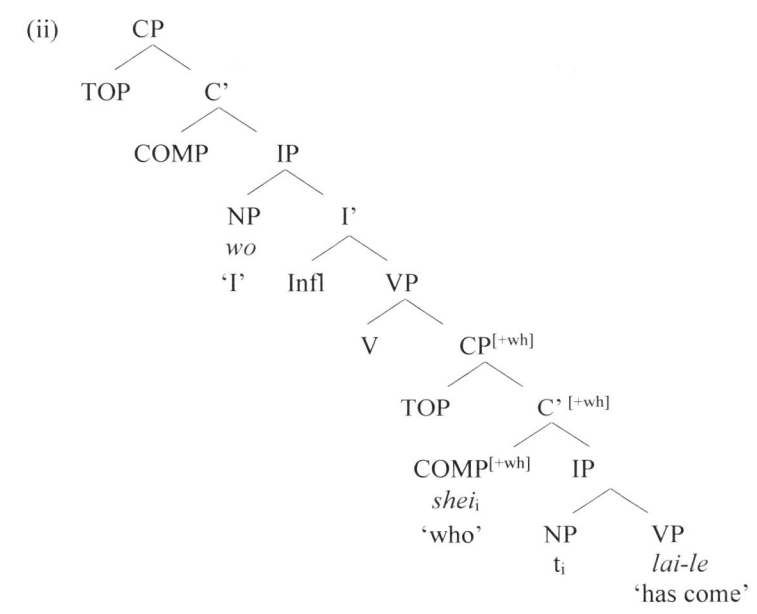

2 Although it is the closest nominal element, the head noun of the relative clause cannot serve as the antecedent to the pro since it is already the antecedent of some other element (i.e. an empty operator). Following Huang (1984) in spirit, we assume that the head noun of a relativized construction that is already co-indexed with some nominal element does not count as a potential antecedent of another empty category.

Chapter **6**

The Interaction of Grammatical Features "Question" and "Focus"[*]

ABSTRACT: *From a UG perspective, there are three grammatical devices to process the grammatical feature "question" or "[+Wh]": moving, adjoining, and reduplicating. There are two devices for a formal grammar to process the grammatical feature "focus" or "[+Focus]": the fronting of a focused constituent and the inserting of a Focus Marker, such as the English "be," before a focused constituent. In this mode of formulation, a set of language-particular and structure-particular grammatical properties, such as those of English interrogative and cleft sentences, and that of Chinese focus construction are decomposed, re-analyzed and significantly simplified. There is no such thing as "Wh-Movement" in a formal theory of English syntax. What is called "Wh-Movement" is shown to be an instantiation of a more generally applicable rule, "Focus-Fronting," in English Wh-questions. The so-called "Question Formation" is thus decomposed into two independent processes: "Subject-Auxiliary Inversion" and "Focus Fronting."*

[*]A version of this chapter originally appeared with the title "the Interaction of the Grammatical Features 'Question' and 'Focus' in Sentences" in *Journal of Chinese Language and Computing* 10:1 (2000), pp. 99–124. Revisions made are technical and minimal, the essential contents remain unchanged. It is included in this monograph as a chapter with kind permission from the Chinese and Oriental Languages Information Processing Society, Singapore.

6.1 Introduction

In the literature, "Focus" related issues have been studied from different perspectives. Following Culicover and Rochemont (1983, 1990) and Horvath (1986), in this paper, we assume that this essentially semantic conception of "Focus" can be characterized as a purely formal syntactic feature [+Focus] or [+F]. This feature gets assigned to various constituents at a certain appropriate level of syntactic representation, participating in syntactic operations under general syntactic principles and constraints. In Section 6.2 we will first review some basic assumptions about the formal characterization of [+F], then move quickly to the question of how [+F] is reflected in the formal syntax, especially how it is marked syntactically. Section 6.3 is devoted to a discussion of the so-called "Focus-Fronting." In particular, we will argue that a constituent with feature [+F] will be fronted in exactly the same fashion in English regardless of whether it is a *Wh*-phrase or not, and that the so-called "Wh-Movement" is, in fact, one instantiation of "Focus-Fronting." This makes the postulation of the former in the grammar essentially redundant. In Section 6.4 we will demonstrate that the cluster of properties normally associated with English "Question-Formation" can be decomposed and simplified. Cleft-sentences and *Wh*-questions in the English language, as well as in many others, have more similarities than differences, and their similarities can be attributed quite naturally to the fact that they both result from the instantiation of a single syntactic rule, as expected. Their differences can be accounted for independently in a modularized theory of grammar. Our major conclusions are summarized briefly in Section 6.5.

6.2 [+Focus] and Its Grammatical Processing

6.2.1 [+Focus]: Some Working Assumptions

It is noted in some early generative literature that one aspect of semantic interpretation of a sentence is a division of its reading into FOCUS and PRESUPPOSITION. As a working definition, we follow Jackendoff (1972) to assume (1) below.

(1) *FOCUS:* The information in the sentence that is assumed by the speaker not to be shared by him and the hearer.

PRESUPPOSITION: The information in the sentence that is assumed by the speaker to be shared by him and the hearer.

According to (1), for a normal sentence, the question is whether the FOCUS or FOCI is/are reflected syntactically or not, rather than whether it has a FOCUS at all. Sentence (2) below, for example, may be analyzed as (3) in terms of FOCUS and PRESUPPOSITION, although it only has phonological, but no syntactic, FOCUS marking (The capitalized word represents the main stress and the highest pitch of the sentence).

(2) Mary hit JOHN.

(3) PRESUPPOSITION: Mary hit someone

   FOCUS: John

The unshared information is assumed by the speaker to be known to the speaker himself in a declarative sentence, whereas it is known to the hearer, but not to the speaker, in an interrogative sentence. For example:

(4) Who did Mary hit?

(5) PRESUPPOSITION: Mary hit someone

   FOCUS: who

Note that Jackendoff's definition of Focus in (1), although quite consistent with intuition, is formulated more semantically or pragmatically than formal-syntactically. Given the line of pursuit adopted in this study, we here would follow Culicover and Rochemont (1983, 1990) and Horvath (1986) to postulate that Focus can also be characterized as a purely formal syntactic feature, [+FOCUS] or [+F], which gets assigned to constituents at an appropriate level of syntactic representation. We will refer to the process of associating the feature [+FOCUS] with a particular constituent as "Focus-Assignment." We assume, leaving arguments and motivations to be offered later, that Focus-Assignment takes place at the level of D-Structure, and not until then does the issue of "Focus" turn into a syntactic one. If so,

(6) below can then be taken as the DS representation of sentence (2) above if the information about "Focus" is to be included.

(6) Mary hit John[+F] .

Although every sentence, by definition, has at least one focused constituent, degree of focalization (i.e. the degree of emphasis) on different constituents may vary from one sentence to another. For expository convenience, we assume that there are two types of Focus that are formal-linguistically relevant: "Strong Focus" and "Weak Focus" (henceforth, "Fs" and "Fw," respectively, when necessary). We assume that this information is also available at the D-Structure to trigger various syntactic and/or phonological processes. Also, given the existence of multiple *wh* questions, a single sentence may have more than one constituent assigned the feature [+FOCUS].

6.2.2 A Device in the Grammatical Processing of [+F]: Focus Marker in Chinese

The [+F] marking resulting from Focus-Assignment may trigger phonological and/or syntactic processing. The phonological processing of [+F], such as primary stress and higher pitch, has been noted in the literature (e.g. Jackendoff (1972), and Culicover and Rochemont (1983), among others). As for syntactic processing, the most conceivable way is simply to insert an overt Focus Marker in the sentence, whatever the marker may be in a particular language. This possibility is attested in Chinese (Xu and Li (1993) and Xu (2001), among others). For example:

(7) Shi wo mingtian cheng huoche qu Guangzhou.
    SHI I   tomorrow ride train   go Guangzhou
    "I will go to Guangzhou by train tomorrow/
    It is I who will go to Guangzhou by train tomorrow."

(8) Wo shi mingtian cheng huoche qu Guangzhou.
    I   SHI tomorrow ride train   go Guangzhou
    "I will go to Guangzhou by train TOMORROW/
    It is tomorrow when I will go to Guangzhou by train."

(9) Wo mingtian shi cheng huoche qu Guangzhou.

    I tomorrow SHI ride train   go Guangzhou

    "I will go to Guangzhou BY TRAIN tomorrow /

    It is by train that I will go to Guangzhou tomorrow."

(10) wo mingtian cheng huoche shi qu Guangzhou.

     I tomorrow ride train   SHI go Guangzhou

    "I will go to GUANGZHOU by train tomorrow/

    It is to Guangzhou that I will go by train tomorrow."

As seen in the above examples, *shi* "to be" is deployed to mark a focused constituent in Chinese. Of course, this is not the only usage of *shi* in the language. *Shi*, just like its English counterpart "to be," may also be a regular copular verb as in *Ta shi yige xuesheng* "He is a student." We may call the *shi* in copular usage "Copular *shi*" and that in emphatic usage "Emphatic *shi*." In terms of parts of speech, *shi* is a verb in both usages. It also should be noted that the status of the emphatic *shi* as a Focus Marker is controversial in the literature. It would seem that Teng (1979) first calls *shi* a "Focus Marker." But, Huang (1989), among others, argues that *shi* cannot be analyzed as a pure Focus Marker, since it exhibits a whole set of features of regular Chinese verbs. For example, it may enter the so-called "V-neg-V" questions, as in (11) below; it can be negated by a negative adverb such as *bu* "not," as in (12). More importantly, argues Huang, the distribution of emphatic *shi* is very much restricted. It can be placed only before the subject NP or somewhere between the subject and the main verb, but never between a verb and its object as in (13) nor between a preposition and its object as in (14).

(11) Shi bu shi ta zuotian   jie-le   ni de shu?

    SHI not SHI he yesterday borrow-Asp your book

    "Was it he who borrowed your book yesterday?"

(12) Ta bu shi guai ni.

    he not SHI blame you

    "He does not blame YOU / It is not you that he blames."

(13) *Wo zuotian zai xuexiao pengjian-le shi ta.

    I   yesterday on campus meet-Asp SHI him

    "Intended: I met HIM on the campus/

    It was him whom I met on the campus yesterday."

(14) *Wo bei shi   ta pian-le.

    I   by SHI him cheat-Asp

    "Intended: I have been cheated by HIM /

    It was him by whom I have cheated."

These observations are true. All they suggest to us, however, is only that *shi* syntactically behaves as a verb while functioning as a Focus Marker, but they don't contradict the claim that *shi* is a Focus Marker. The initial purpose of inserting *shi* may well be just to mark the focused constituent. After being inserted into the sentence, however, *shi* takes up its own way of life, exhibiting a set of properties of regular copular verbs. This is expected. Putting it in different words, we can say that the ungrammaticality of sentences like (13) and (14) has nothing to do with the insertion of *shi* as a Focus Marker. Rather, they are ungrammatical because such verbs as *pengjian* "meet" may only have an NP, but not a VP, as its complement. In short, seen from a different perspective, *shi* could be different things in different contexts. In terms of the grammatical processing of [+F], *shi* is a Focus Marker. In terms of parts of speech, it is simply a verb. In deploying this lexical item *shi* as a Focus Marker, the grammar automatically places it under the constraint of the conditions which govern verbs in general.

Theoretically, every sentence has at least one focused constituent. Superficially, some sentences don't appear to have a focused constituent. In fact, it may be the case that they don't have a presupposition and the whole sentence, or at least its predicate, could be the focused constituent. It is commonly known that not all Chinese sentences employ the Focus Marker *shi* to mark the constituent. Here, the division between Strong and Weak Focus proposed earlier in this chapter plays a crucial role in determining whether a focused constituent is syntactically processed through the insertion of the Focus Marker *shi* in Chinese. Suppose that all focused constituents are somehow phonologically reflected in the component of

Phonetic Form (PF). The formal syntax is sensitive only to the feature of [+Fs] (Strong Focus). Assuming that *zai bangongshi li* "in the office" is the focused constituent in both (15) and (16) below, and that it is strong in (15), but weak in (16), we can analyze them at different levels of representation as follows.

(15) DS: Wo zuotian [zai bangongshi li]$^{[+Fs]}$ deng ni.
     SS: Wo zuotian shi [zai bangongshi li]$^{[+Fs]}$ deng ni
     PF: Wo zuotian SHI ZAI BANGONGSHI LI deng ni.
        I   yesterday SHI in office   wait-for you
        "I waited for you IN THE OFFICE yesterday/
        It was in the office that I waited for you yesterday."

(16) DS: Wo zuotian [zai bangongshi li]$^{[+Fw]}$ deng ni.
     SS: Wo zuotian [zai bangongshi li]$^{[+Fw]}$ deng ni
     PF: Wo zuotian ZAI BANGONGSHI LI deng ni.
        I   yesterday SHI in office   wait-for you
        "I waited for you IN THE OFFICE yesterday."

We propose that the insertion of Focus Marker *shi* is triggered by the [+Fs] marking from the DS representation. The process of Focus Marker insertion, we assume, is an instance of Adjoin-α in the sense of Lebeaux (1991), which, along with Move-α and Project-α, takes place in the course of derivation of SS from DS, as in (17) (Lebeaux (1991)).

(17) DS

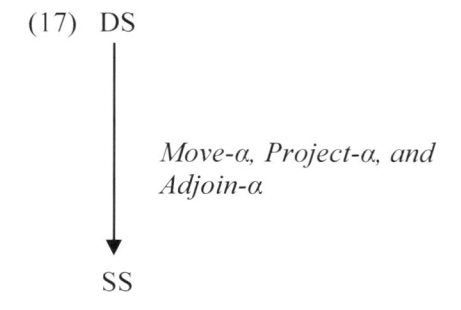

      SS

This proposal amounts to saying that the Focus Marker *shi* is not present at DS, but gets adjoined-in later in the course of derivation. According to

Lebeaux's Principle of Licensing Well-Formedness, defined in (18), for an element to be present in the phrase marker, it has to be properly licensed, perhaps in different ways for different grammatical elements. An element cannot be present until the relevant licensing relation allowing or requiring it in the phrase marker has applied.

(18) PRINCIPLE OF LICENSING WELL-FORMEDNESS (UG)

A subtree Ts may not appear in a major tree Tm prior to the point in the derivation that Ts is licensed in Tm (Ts, Tm relative).

Note that neither the Projection Principle nor anything else requires the presence of *shi* in the DS representation. *Shi*, as an emphatic verb, has to be analyzed as not participating in the Argument Structure, otherwise the obvious similarities among sentences (7), (8), (9), and (10) above, which differ in nothing but Focus-Marking, cannot be properly captured. We assume that these sentences share the same common DS representation in terms of the basic structure, but have different assignments of [+Fs], the later eventually triggers the insertion of the Focus Marker *shi* before different constituents, perhaps to satisfy an SS condition like (19) below.

(19) A constituent with [+Fs] marking must be reflected with Focus Marker *shi* at SS in Chinese.

Also note that the Focus Marker *shi* is absent at DS. The [+Fs] marking, however, has to be assigned and/or checked at the DS level to provide proper triggering for the insertion of *shi*. This proposal represents a nontrivial departure from those of Jackendoff (1972), Chomsky (1981), and Horvath (1986), who all explicitly or implicitly assume that Focus Assignment takes place at SS. One reason that forbids the adoption of the SS-Focus-Assignment approach is that it creates a dilemma in handling the Chinese case, since if it were the case, *shi* would have to pre-exist at DS because the necessary triggering that calls for its insertion would not be available before SS. We know it cannot be there, though, because its licensing takes place at SS. Additional arguments will be provided for our DS-Focus-Assignment approach as we proceed.

The placement of the Focus Marker *shi* in linear word order is determined jointly by two factors. [1] As a verb in terms of part of speech, *shi* has to observe all relevant syntactic conditions governing verbs in Chinese. For example, it cannot be inserted between a verb and its object, even if the object NP has a [+Fs] mark from DS representation. In this case, *shi* normally is placed immediately before the verb. [2] *Shi* is to be placed as close as possible to the focused constituent in a sentence, should applicable conditions allow for this.

A single sentence, as noted above, may have two or more focused constituents. Now it should be pointed out that only one of the several focused constituents can be marked overtly with *shi*. The following sentences are unacceptable.

(20) *Wo shi zuotian shi zai bangongshi li deng ni.
　　　I　SHI yesterday SHI in office　　wait-for you
　　　"Intended Meaning: I waited for you IN THE OFFICE
　　　YESTERDAY."

(21) *Shi wo shi mei mai na ben shu.
　　　SHI I　SHI not buy that　book
　　　"Intended Meaning: It was I who did not buy THAT BOOK."

To account for this phenomenon, a condition on Focus-Assignment is proposed in Xu and Li (1993) as defined in (22) below.

(22) The Unique Strong Focus Condition
　　　A simplex sentence can only have one constituent assigned a Strong Focus Mark [+Fs].

If this is so, then we can say that the Unique Strong Focus Condition is violated in (20) and (21), making them ungrammatical. Also note that (22) should be taken as a condition on a clause, i.e. an unembedded simplex sentence. A sentence with an embedded clause, of course, may have two or more strongly focused constituents, and consequently may have two or more constituents syntactically marked with *shi*. For example:

(23) Shi Zhangsan zhidao [shi Lisi dasui-le nage beizi].
SHI Zhangsan know SHI Lisi break-Asp that cup
"It is Zhangsan who knows that it is Lisi who broke the cup."

In *wh*-questions, only the *wh*-phrase, not any others, can be the strongly focused constituent. With further arguments to be provided later, we assume that this is because *wh*-phrases have already been assigned the Strong Focus mark [+Fs] in the lexicon and carry the mark into syntax when they themselves are composed into a phrase marker. Such a lexical marking interacts with the syntactic marking in an interesting way. For example:

(24) Shui$^{[+Fs]}$ mai-le neiben zidian?
who   buy-Asp that dictionary
"Who bought that dictionary?"

(25) Ni shenme shihou$^{[+Fs]}$ nian-de daxue?
you what   time   attend-Asp college
"When did you attend college?"

If necessary, the Focus Marker *shi* may also be inserted to intensify focus marking, giving rise to sentences like the following.

(24') Shi shui$^{[+Fs]}$ mai-le neiben zidian?
SHI who   buy-Asp that dictionary
"WHO bought that dictionary?"

(25') Ni shi shenme shihou$^{[+Fs]}$ nian-de daxue?
you SHI what   time   attend-Asp college
"WHEN did you attend college?"

In the event a *wh*-phrase is in an object position, the Focus Marker will have to be placed before the main verb rather than before the *wh* object.

(26) Zhangsan shi mai-le shenme$^{[+Fs]}$?
Zhangsan SHI buy-Asp what
"WHAT did Zhangsan buy?"

The constituents with the [+Fs] mark in sentences (24'), (25'), and (26) can be taken as having a double focus marking. One is brought in along with the *wh*-phrase from the lexicon, and another obtained through a syntactic process, namely the insertion of Focus Marker *shi*. This kind of double focus marking is allowed in Chinese, but not in English. We will return to this issue in Section 6.4.2.

The Unique Strong Focus Condition, as specified in (22), which disallows a single clause to have more than one strongly focused constituent and the assumption that *wh*-phrases are assigned [+Fs] in the lexicon so that they carry the mark inherently, together lead to a prediction: The Focus Marker *shi* can be inserted only to mark the *wh*-phrases in *wh*-questions. This prediction is borne out in Chinese, as seen from the ungrammaticality of the following sentences.

(27) *Shi Zhangsan$^{[+Fs]}$ pian-le shui$^{[+Fs]}$?
    SHI Zhangsan   cheat-Asp who
    "Intended: *Is it Zhangsan who has cheated who?/
    Who has ZHANGSAN cheated?"

(28) *Ni shenme shihou$^{[+Fs]}$ shi zai Meiguo$^{[+Fs]}$ gongzuo?
    you what   time   SHI in America   work
    "Intended: When did you work IN AMERICA?"

(29) *Shui$^{[+Fs]}$ shi mai-le nenme duo shu$^{[+Fs]}$?
    who   SHI buy-Asp so many book
    "Intended: Who bought SO MANY BOOKS?"

The ungrammaticality of the above sentences may present a puzzle for an alternative analysis of the Focus Assignment, since the Focus Marker *shi*, in general, may be inserted to mark any constituent that is strongly focused in a sentence. Given that the Unique Strong Focus Condition is independently motivated, the phenomenon can be taken as a strong argument for our assumption that the *wh*-phrase is marked [+Fs] in the lexicon and carries the mark along into the syntax. In short, syntactic marking and lexical marking of strong focus must coincide.

6.3 Focus-Fronting

Cross-linguistically, the insertion of a Focus Marker may just represent one way of syntactically processing a strong focus. An alternative device is to move the focused constituent to a more prominent position. In most cases, the constituent is preposed. This is called "Focus-Fronting," which is observed in such languages as Archaic Chinese, Hungarian, and English.

6.3.1 Focus-Fronting in Archaic Chinese

The basic word order of Archaic Chinese, just like that of modern Chinese, is of S-V-O. For example:

(30) Wan   min   pi   qi li. (Mozi, Shangxian Zhong)
ten-thousand people receive its benefit
"Thousands of people benefit from it."

(31) Qin wang fu   ji   ke. (Zhanguoce, Yance)
Qin king again attack Ke
"The King of Qin attacked Ke again."

As noted widely in the literature, an object NP may be preposed to a pre-verbal position under certain conditions. The best characterization of the so-called "Object-Preposing" in Archaic Chinese can be found in Wang (1958), wherein the following patterns are identified.

[1] Object NPs that are question words (i.e. *wh*-phrases) must be fronted. For example:

(32) Wu <u>shui</u> qi?   qi tian hu? (Lun Yu. Zihan)
I   who cheat   cheat God Q-Particle
"Who do I cheat? Do (I) cheat the God?"

(33) Chen shi bu cai, you <u>shui</u> gan yuan (Zuozhuan. Chenggong Year 3)
I   really not talented, so who dare blame
"I am really not talented. Who do (I) dare to blame?"

[2] Object NPs in negative sentences may or may not be fronted as in (34), (35), and (36).

(34) Riyue shi yi, sui bu <u>wo</u> yu (Lun Yu. Yanghuo)
time pass Asp year not me wait-for
"Time flies. Time won't wait for me."

(35) Wo wu <u>er</u> zha, er wu <u>wo</u> yu. (Zuozhuan, Xuangong Year 15)
I not you cheat you not me cheat
"I won't cheat you, and you better not cheat me."

(36) Shenren bu ai <u>ji</u>. (Sunzi. Zhengming)
holy-person not love self
"The holy people don't love themselves."

[3] Emphatic NPs must be fronted.

(37) Jun .... <u>qun chen</u> shi you. (Zuozhuan. Xigong Year 15)
King   those ministers that concern
"The King .... concerns THOSE MINISTERS."

(38) Yu wei li shi shi. (Zuozhuan. Chenggong Year 15)
I only interest that care
"I care about INTEREST only."

Most authors, including Wang (1958), attempt to relate this kind of "Object-Preposing" to the formation of question and negation. Note that this kind of structure-particular approach leaves a major question unresolved: What do those interrogative, negative and emphatic sentences that eventually get their object NPs fronted have in common? Another puzzling fact is that all *wh*-object NPs in questions, but only some object NPs in negative sentences get fronted. Taking a different line of approach, we here would propose that these superficially unrelated sentence patterns are all derived through one single syntactic process: The fronting of strongly focused constituents. As a first approximation, we propose (39).

(39) Move those constituents with [+Fs] marking to a pre-verbal position in Archaic Chinese.

Under this proposal, the observed "Object-Preposing" phenomena can all be accounted for quite neatly. *Wh*-phrases, as argued above, are all marked [+Fs] in the lexicon and they carry this mark into the syntax. Also, as proposed in Xu and Li (1993) on an independent ground, negative adverbs have dual functions: Negating and Focusing. In case the object NP in a negative sentence happens to be a focused constituent, its degree of focalization will be intensified by a negative adverb and will become higher. Furthermore, an object NP in a regular, non-interrogative and non-negative sentence can still be assigned the mark [+Fs] through Focus Assignment. In short, the above "Object-Preposing" constructions all have their object NPs marked [+Fs] in different ways and at different levels. (32), (35), and (38), for example, can be postulated as (32'), (35'), and (38') respectively at DS.

(32') Wu qi shui$^{[+Fs]}$?   qi tian hu?
     I cheat who   cheat God Q-Particle

(35') Wo wu zha er$^{[+Fs]}$, er wu yu wo$^{[+Fs]}$.
     I not cheat you   you not cheat me

(38') Yu wei shi shi.   li$^{[+Fs]}$.
     I only that care interest

It is now not surprising at all that the object NP is preposed only in some negative sentences, but remains in a post-verbal position in others. Negative adverbs will intensify the focus, but what is being intensified does not have to be the object NP. It may well be, say, the subject NP. If the subject NP is strongly focused, the object NP, of course, will not be preposed. To generalize, we can say that the "Object-Preposing" phenomena are directly related neither to question nor to negation. Rather, it is related to focus. This point can best be illustrated as follows.

Because ↓	*Then* ↓	
Wh-question	Assignment of Feature [+Fs]	Fronting of Constituent with Feature [+Fs]
Negation		
Emphasis		
	Because ↑	*Then* ↑

An obvious question regarding the movement account of the above phenomena is where the focused constituent moves. That is, where is the landing site? To answer this question, we would like to appeal to a proposal made by Larson (1988) with regard to the VP complement in the double object construction. Details aside, one of Larson's important claims is that a VP may consist of an empty V position (i.e. a VP shell) that takes another VP as a complement. Under this proposal, the VP structure underlying a double object construction like (40), for example, will be postulated as (41). From their respective DS positions, the verb *send*, as driven by the Case assignment and tense/agreement requirements, raises up into the empty V position, and *Mary*, to receive Case assignment, moves to the "subject" position of the complement VP in a fashion that Larson identifies with passivization.

(40) John sent Mary a letter. (Larson (1988:25))

(41)

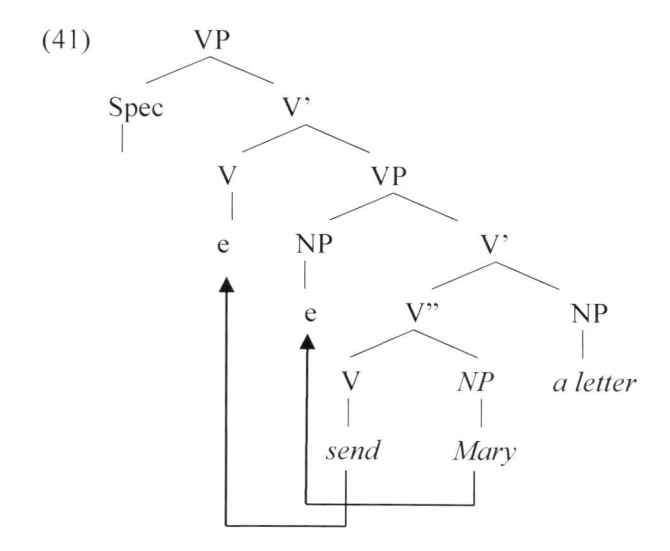

Note that there is no principled reason that the VP structure that Larson postulates for the double object construction would be limited to that particular type of construction. Taking this a step further, we would assume that it is available generally to various types of transitive constructions, including the one under consideration here. If so, we can now say that the

VP structure underlying sentences like (38), repeated below as (42), is (43). And from its DS position, *li* "benefit" moves into the higher NP position as an instance of substitution.

(42) Yu wei li shi shi. (Zuozhuan. Chenggong Year 15)
     I only interest that care
     "I care about INTEREST only."

(43)

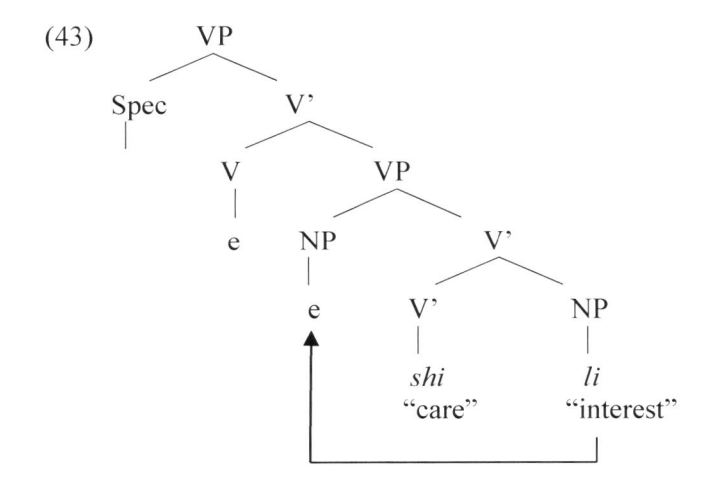

The verb in Archaic Chinese, unlike its counterpart in the English double object construction, does not raise into the empty V position after the NP has been moved. Recall that the primary motivation for V-Raising in the English double object construction is the Case requirement of the moved NP. Suppose that such verbs as *send* can only assign one structural Accusative Case, which has been assigned to the NP *in situ, a letter*. For *Mary* to be saved from a Case Filter violation, *send* has to raise up to assign a Case to it, leaving behind a verbal trace to assign Case to the unmoved NP *a letter*. But if "Focus-Fronting" is a type of A'-movement, we can say that the moved NP in Archaic Chinese inherits the Case-Assignment property from its trace. If so, then there will be no motivation triggering V-Raising in the language, and the verb thus remains *in situ*. The higher empty V position remains empty throughout the derivation.

Another problem still requires an explanation. Note that an object NP can be assigned an Accusative Case in the post-verbal position. The problem is why the NP moves at all. Our answer is that there is an S-Structure condition, as formulated in (44), which triggers such a movement.

(44) An NP with the strong focus mark [+Fs] must terminate in a Focus Position.

In the particular language of Archaic Chinese, the Focus Position is the pre-verbal position, after subject, if there is one. As will be illustrated later, this is just one of the options available in UG.

6.3.2 Focus-Fronting in Hungarian

Similar phenomena are also observed in Hungarian, as reported in Horvath (1986) among others. In terms of the basic word order, Hungarian is also an S-V-O language, e.g.

(45) Attila felt a foldrengestol.
Attila feared the earthquake-from
"Attila was afraid of the earthquake."

(46) Mari az asztalra tette az edenyeket.
Mary the table-onto put the dishes-Acc
"Mary put the dishes on the table."

(47) Janos megcafolta a professzor erveit.
John   refuted-3sg the professor argument-3sg-Poss-Pl-Acc
"John refuted the professor's argument."

(48) A fiuk   mind   legyoztek Marit.
the boys-Nom all-Nom defeated-3pl Mary-Acc
"The boys all defeated Mary."

If an object NP is a *wh*-phrase or a focused constituent, it will not remain in a post-verbal position. Rather, it has to move to a pre-verbal position, otherwise the sentence will be ungrammatical.

(49) Attila A FOLDRENGESTOL$_i$ felt t$_i$.

    Attila the earthquake-from feared

    "Attila was afraid of THE EARTHQUAKE/

    It was the earthquake that Attila was afraid of ."

(50) Mari mit$_i$ telt az asztalra t$_i$?

    Mary what-Acc put the table-onto

    "What did Mary put on the table?"

(51) Mari kinek$_i$ vett   egy   konyvet t$_i$ ajandekba?

    Mary who-to bought-3sg a book-Acc   present-into

    "Who did Mary buy a book for as a present?"

(52) *Attila felt A FOLDRENGESTOL.

    Attila feared the earthquake-from

(53) *Mari telt az asztalra mit?

    Mary put the table-onto what-Acc

The movement exhibited in the above sentences is also triggered by the strong focus mark [+Fs] in Hungarian in the same way as in Archaic Chinese to satisfy an SS condition, such as (44). It is interesting to note that the formal syntax of Hungarian is not sensitive to whether a focused constituent is a *wh*-phrase or not. It will move as long as it has the mark [+Fs]. Rather, it is sensitive only to whether the mark is strong "[+Fs]" or weak "[+Fw]." The only difference is that mark [+Fs] is assigned to *wh*-phrases in the lexicon and to non-*wh*-phrases in syntax at the DS level. It is reasonable therefore to take (54) and (55) below as the corresponding DS representations for (49) and (50). Another important point that should be made clear here is that the mark [+Fs] won't be deleted after triggering the fronting movement. Rather, it has to remain there, as the focused constituents have to be identifiable both in the LF component to ensure the correct semantic interpretation and in the FP component to trigger appropriate assignment of primary stress and intonation peak.

(54) Attila felt   a   foldrengestol[+Fs].
     Attila feared the earthquake-from

(55) Mari telt az asztalra mit[+Fs]?
     Mary put the table-onto what-Acc

6.3.3 The English Cleft-Sentence

As demonstrated in the sections above, cross-linguistically there are two types of syntactic processing of [+Fs]-marked constituents. One is "Focus Marking," which inserts a Focus Marker (e.g. the copular verb *shi*) before the strongly focused constituent, as attested in modern Chinese, and the other is "Focus-Fronting," which moves the strongly focused constituent to a pre-verbal position, as observed in Archaic Chinese and modern Hungarian. Now it makes sense to question whether these two devices can be jointly employed in a single construction from a single language. Theoretically, there is nothing in principle that disallows this possibility. In this section, we propose that the formation of the English cleft-sentences is an instantiation of this logical possibility. Consider the following examples.

(56) It is the new house$_i$ that John will buy t$_i$ for his mother tomorrow.

(57) It is tomorrow$_i$ when John will buy the new house for his mother t$_i$.

(58) It is for his mother$_i$ that John will buy the new house t$_i$ tomorrow.

(59) It is John$_i$ t$_i$ who will buy the new house for his mother tomorrow.

Our proposal is that sentences in (56)–(59) have a common DS representation in terms of the basic syntactic structure and differ minimally in the assignment of focus. For example:

(56') John will buy the new house[+Fs] for his mother tomorrow.

(57') John will buy the new house for his mother tomorrow[+Fs].

(58') John will buy the new house for his mother[+Fs] tomorrow.

(59') John[+Fs] will buy the new house for his mother tomorrow.

To process the feature [+Fs] syntactically, English employs two devices: "Focus-Fronting" and "Focus Marking." The Focus Marker in English, interestingly, is also a copular verb *to be*. These two devices are both triggered by the same feature mark [+Fs] and both take place in the course of derivation of SS from DS. Since a complementizer such as *that* always co-occurs with the moved focused constituents, it is reasonable to assume that the landing site of focused constituents is Spec/CP. Also, although evidence does not strongly indicate the application order of the two devices, we assume that "Focus Marking" takes place before "Focus-Fronting." In short, we postulate (60) as the derivational course for an English cleft-sentence such as (56).

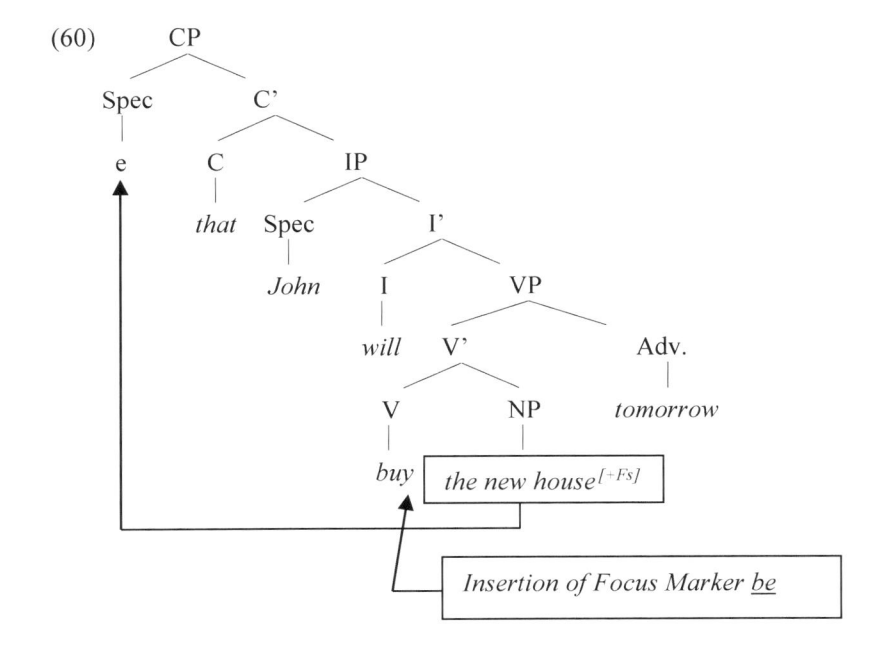

This movement approach to the analysis of the English cleft-sentences may represent a non-trivial departure from the traditional analysis, and some justifications are thus in order. For us, the following properties of this type of sentences, which could remain unexplained by a non-movement account, all argue for the movement approach.

[1] These sentences all have a sentence-internal and co-referential gap, and this gap may be rewritten as the *wh*-resumptive pronoun *who*.

[2] The movement, very much like that in Hungarian noted above, can apply over an apparently unbounded domain. For example:

(61) It is the new house$_i$ that I think t$_i$ (that) John will buy t$_i$ for his mother tomorrow.

(62) It is for his mother$_i$ that I believe t$_i$ (that) John will buy this new house t$_i$ tomorrow.

[3] The movement is also under the constraint of the relevant Locality conditions. For example, it cannot move a constituent out of a complex NP, as shown in the following sentences.

(63) *It is the earthquake$_i$ that Bill heard [$_{NP}$ the news that Cathy had been afraid of t$_i$]

(64) *It is the new house$_i$ that John knows [$_{NP}$ his brother's promise that he will buy t$_i$ for his mother].

[4] The focused NP inherits Case assignment from its post-verbal trace. The following variation in overt Case-marking is expected under a movement approach, and it will be unexplained otherwise.

(65) It is he/*him who likes Mary.

(66) It is him/*he whom Mary likes.

Note that the English Focus Marker *to be* is also a copular verb. As discussed above, a Focus Marker must fall under a certain part of speech, so it must observe the relevant conditions that other members of its part of speech observe. *Shi* behaves just like a regular copular verb while functioning as a Focus Marker. This is also the case for the English *to be*. After being inserted into the sentence, *to be* behaves just like a regular copular verb. For instance, it may be inflected for tense, as in (67), and may exchange positions with the subject NP in questions (i.e. "Subject-Auxiliary Inversion'), as in (68).

(67) It was your cat that I found in the park.

(68) Is it Bill that Mary hates?

There seems to be a salient difference between English and Chinese in the insertion of Focus Marker. It is clear in Chinese that what is inserted as a focus marker is just *shi*, but in English what is inserted before focused constituents seems to be *it is*. We propose that the Focus Marker in English as well as in Chinese is the copular verb *shi/be*. The existence of expletive *it* has nothing to do with either focus or focus marking. Rather, the insertion of *it* is due to a completely different requirement of the English grammar which, presumably as an effect of the Null Subject Parameter setting, requires the subject position be filled with a lexical NP. In other words, expletive *it* has to be inserted there for the same reason that requires insertion of the same expletive pronoun in (69), (70), and (71).

(69) It is raining.

(70) It seems that John will buy the new house.

(71) It is assumed that John will buy the new house.

Given that the insertion of *it* is due to a motivation completely independent of Focus and Focus Marking, we should not be surprised if somebody says that there is a language which, unlike English, employs the two syntactic devices of Focus-Processing, but, unlike English, allows null subjects.

The cluster of properties that one normally relates to the formation of the English cleft-sentences now has been decomposed and made to follow from independently motivated principles. We take this feature of the approach as a simplification of the grammar. This is a welcome result in the spirit of the modular theory of grammar. Superficially, the syntactic devices in processing strongly focused constituents appear to be very much different from one language to another. Now we can see, however, that those cross-linguistic facts have resulted from the choice between only two possible devices (a very limited number of options) in interaction with independently motivated principles and/or language-particular properties.

Archaic Chinese and modern Hungarian, on one hand, and modern English on the other differ minimally in the landing sites of the focused constituents. Recall that the focused constituents in Archaic Chinese and modern Hungarian move to a pre-verbal position, i.e. the Spec position of a complement VP, while their counterparts in English move to the Spec position of a CP. Obviously, why there is such a cross-linguistic difference is an interesting question. We leave this question open, but point out that this difference may also be due to a reason independent of focus and explainable in a modular theory of grammar.

6.4 *"Wh*-Movement" as Focus-Fronting

Our proposal is that the movement of focused constituents is triggered by the strong focus mark [+Fs] for both *Wh*-phrases and non-*Wh*-phrases. *Wh*-phrases and non-*Wh*-phrases differ minimally in how and where the mark [+Fs] is assigned, but not in whether the mark is assigned nor in whether the [+Fs]-marked constituents will move. [+Fs] is assigned to *Wh*-phrases in the lexicon and is carried along the *Wh*-phrases into the syntax, where it is assigned to non-*Wh*-phrases at DS through "Focus-Assignment." The formal syntax is sensitive only to whether a certain constituent is so marked, but not to where and how it is marked. If this approach is correct, we are in a position to say that the widely recognized, structure-particular "*Wh*-Movement" rule can be subsumed under the general "Focus-Fronting" rule, and there is no such thing as "*Wh*-Movement" in the formal syntax.

The above unified account of *wh*-questions and cleft sentences works straightforwardly in Archaic Chinese and modern Hungarian, as there is virtually no difference between Focus-Fronting of *Wh*-phrases and that of non-Wh-phrases. However, there appears to be an obvious problem when we take a second look at the English phenomenon. As demonstrated above, the formation of English cleft-sentences involves the joint application of two focus devices: The insertion of the Focus Marker *to be*, and the fronting of the focused constituents. The formation of *Wh*-questions, however, seems to involve only the fronting of the *Wh*-phrase, but no insertion of a Focus Marker. Also, the subject NP and the auxiliary verb are inverted in Wh-questions, but not in cleft-sentence. In this section, we shall argue that the differences between *Wh*-questions and cleft-sentences in English can either be accounted for independently or made to follow from a minimal and reasonable assumption. There is not a principled contrast between "Focus-Fronting" and "*Wh*-Movement" in Hungarian and Chinese or in English. The former is an instantiation of the latter. We will start our discussion with a brief review of the relationship between question formation and *Wh*-Movement, since they have been widely assumed in the literature, explicitly or implicitly, to be inherently related.

6.4.1 Decomposing "Question-Formation"

There is a salient difference between interrogative and declarative sentences in the English language. The subject NP and the auxiliary verb have to be inverted in interrogatives, but not in declaratives. Additionally, some interrogatives undergo *Wh*-Movement. These differences are often related to "question-formation." To make our discussion more concrete, it is necessary first to make it clear what "question-formation" refers to. Consider the following two questions.

(72) Will you buy the new house?

(73) What will you buy?

The DS representation of these two interrogatives can be postulated as (74) and (75) respectively below, whereby some kind of abstract question morpheme [+Wh] is included. Crucially, the abstract question morpheme, as a functional category, is a property of the whole CP, rather than that of any lexical constituent in the CP. As a working hypothesis, people normally assume that this property of the CP results from a percolating of the same property from its head, C. Also, the *Wh*-phrase *what* in sentence (73) should be marked [+Fs] in the lexicon and carries the mark into the phrase marker.

(74)

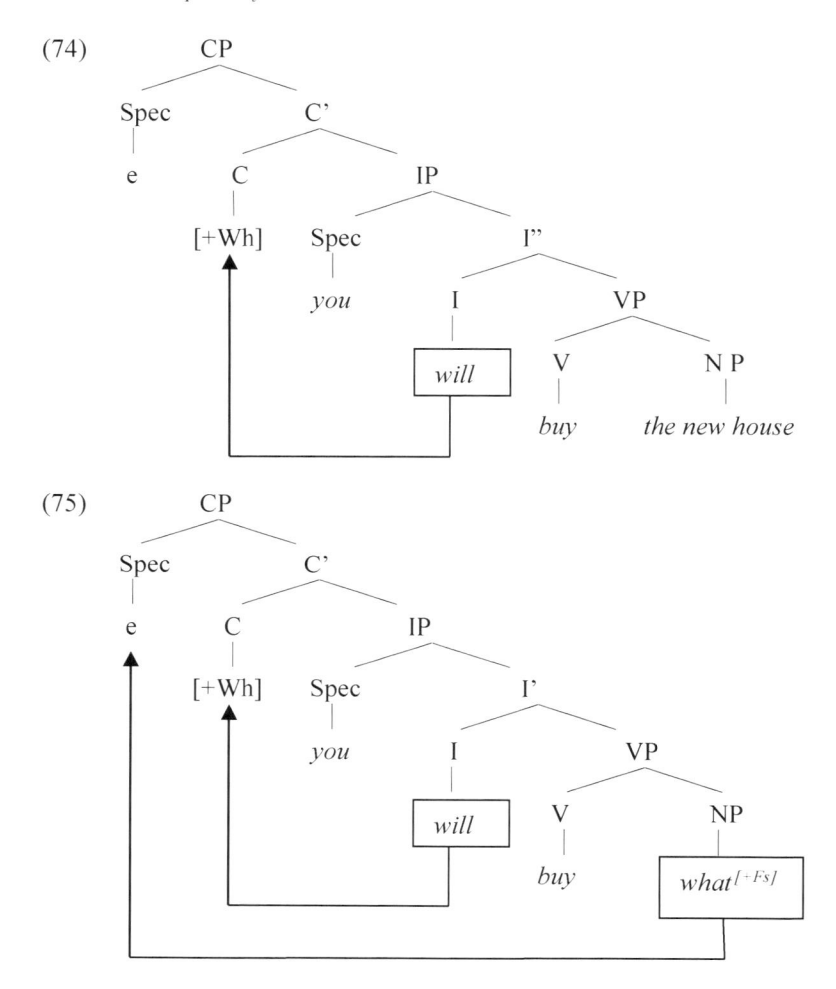

(75)

For a representation like (74) to surface, the auxiliary *will* has to move to the C position, while in (75), *what* also has to move into the Spec/CP position after the movement of the auxiliary *will*. (75) involves two steps of movement while (74) involves only one. What they have in common is the presence of the abstract question morpheme [+Wh] at DS and the application of "Subject-Auxiliary Inversion." Since there is a systematic correlation between the two, it must be that the former that triggers the latter. It should be clear that "the formation of questions" in English is simply the application of a syntactic process, "Subject-Auxiliary Inversion." The movement of the Wh-phrase *what* in (75) has nothing to do with question formation. Rather, it is triggered by a strong focus mark [+Fs] on completely independent grounds that is assigned in the lexicon. As argued above, any constituent marked [+Fs], regardless of whether it is a *Wh*-phrase or not, has to move to the position Spec/CP in English. In other words, sentences like (73) result from the joint application of two syntactic processes — the syntactic process of [+Fs] (i.e. "Focus-Fronting" in English) and that of [+Wh] (i.e. "Subject-Auxiliary Inversion" in English) — and they are completely independent of each other. In contrast, sentences like (72) result only from the application of a single syntactic process — the process of [+Wh] — as no constituent of it is marked [+Fs]. Let us look at another related example.

(76) Is it <u>the new house</u>$_i$ that you will buy t$_i$?

(76) is like (73) in the sense that it is also derived from the joint application of "Focus-Fronting" and "Subject-Auxiliary Inversion." Unlike (73), however, (76) is not a *Wh*-question. Interestingly, the auxiliary being inverted is the inserted Focus Marker *is*, but not *will*, which suggests to us that Focus Marker insertion and Focus-Fronting both apply before Subject-Auxiliary Inversion in English, indicating that the former prompts the latter.

The cluster of properties that are normally related to "question formation" have been successfully decomposed, with "*Wh*-Movement" being recast as an instantiation of "Focus-Fronting," which is completely independent of questions, and "Subject-Auxiliary Inversion," which is analyzed as the only syntactic process triggered by the abstract question morpheme [+Wh]. Subject-Auxiliary Inversion indiscriminately applies to all types of interrogatives, including yes-no questions and *Wh*-questions.

For this decompositional approach, an interesting argument can be constructed based on some language facts observed in the Early English grammar. As noted in Hyams (1986) and Weinberg (1991), the acquisition of the so-called "*Wh*-Movement" in English occurs significantly earlier than that of Subject-Auxiliary Inversion. While the former may be observed in the speech of children 28 months or younger, the latter is rarely seen in the speech of children until they are around 38 months old. The following sentences have been collected from the speech of children around 28 months old (Hyams (1986)).

(77) What doing?   (Cf: What are you doing?)

(78) What cowboy doing? (Cf: What is the cowboy doing?)

As expected, children of 28–38 months old often produce sentences like (79) and (80) below, in which only "*Wh*-Movement" has applied, but Subject-Auxiliary Inversion has not (Data from Weinberg (1991)).

(79) What you are gonna wear? (Adult: What are you going to wear?)

(80) What the mouse is doing? (Adult: What is the mouse doing?)

For us, the difference in sequence of acquisition timing suggests that Subject-Auxiliary Inversion, as the English process triggered by [+Wh], and "*Wh*-Movement," as the English process triggered by [+Fs], are treated independently, and are thus acquired independently, confirming our proposal that they are different in nature. Given that "*Wh*-Movement" is just an instantiation of Focus-Fronting, a prediction can be made here that Focus-Fronting in English cleft-sentences should also be acquired at around 28 months old, and children of 28–38 months old may produce "wrong" questions like (81) below.

(81) (It is) John you know? (Adult: Is it John that you know?)

6.4.2 Deriving the Superficial Contrast between *Wh*-Focus and Non-*Wh*-Focus in English

There is a contrast between *Wh*-focus and non-*Wh*-focus in English. It is noted above that in English there is a joint application of the two focus-processing devices: the insertion of Focus Marker *to be* and the movement of the focused constituent. However, it has to be pointed out that this is the case only in cleft sentences with non-*Wh*-focus. In *Wh*-questions, there is only movement of focused constituent, but no insertion of Focus Marker. This contrast demands an explanation from our proposal, under which

"*Wh*-Movement" and regular "Focus-Fronting" are unified. To pose the question more concretely, why should sentences (84) and (85), which also have a Focus Marker, be ungrammatical while (82) and (83) are acceptable sentences?

(82) Is it <u>the new house</u>$_i$ that you will buy t_i ?

(83) Is it <u>John</u> $_i$ who$_i$ will buy the new house?

(84) *Is it <u>what</u>$_i$ (that) you will buy t_i ?

(85) *It is <u>what</u>$_i$ will you buy t_i ?

If we take cleft-sentences, such as (82) and (83), as the canonical case of syntactic processing of [+Fs] in English, then the question is why *Wh*-questions don't allow the Focus Marker be inserted. To tackle this problem, here we would make a language-particular claim for English. We claim that *Wh*-phrases themselves represent a sort of overt Focus Marking (Let us call it "F-wh'), which is comparable to *be* in English ([F-be]) at an abstract level. Under this proposal, an enriched specification of sentences (86) and (87) at an abstract level will be (86') and (87') respectively. In these new specifications, they both have overt Focus Marking: [F-be] in (86) and [F-wh] in (87). The [F-be] mark is rewritten phonologically as *is*, whereas the [F-wh] mark is incorporated into the *Wh*-word *what* itself.

(86) It is the new house that I will buy.

(87) What will you buy?

(86') [F-be] <u>the new house</u>$_i$ that I will buy t_i.

(87') [F-wh] <u>what</u>$_i$ (that) you will buy t_i.

To generate a sentence like (84), repeated as (88) below, an abstract representation like (89) as a base form will be needed, whereby. In this form, it has a double marking for the focused constituent: [F-wh] and [F-be].

(88) *Is it <u>what</u>$_i$ (that) you will buy t$_i$?

(89) [F-be] [F-wh] what$_i$ (that) you will buy t$_i$.

We can now say that (84) and (85) are ungrammatical because they have two overt markings on focused constituents, and the English grammar does not allow double overt focus marking, presumably as an effect of the redundancy avoidance requirement. Recall that in modern Chinese, the Focus Marker *shi* can be inserted before question words as well as non-question words indiscriminately, so the redundancy avoidance requirement may be a language-particular one.

6.4.3 A Language Typology

We now can generalize to say that there are two devices provided in the UG to process those constituents with the feature [+Fs]: to insert a copular verb *be* as a Focus Marker before a focused constituent, and to move the focused constituent to a more prominent position. Under the constraint of general principles and language-particular requirements, a particular language will make a choice between the two options or simply employ both of the two devices. Three types of languages are attested in terms of how the feature mark [+Fs] is syntactically processed. Figure 1 below could be considered a language typology.

Figure 1

Focus - Marking	*Focus - Fronting*
Modern Chinese	Archaic Chinese, Modern Hungarian
Modern English	

The syntactic processing triggered by [+Fs] is under the constraint of the general grammatical principles and conditions. The Chinese Focus Marker *shi*, for instance, is also a verb while functioning as a Focus Marker. Because of this, the grammar must ensure that it will observe the conditions that are applicable to verbs in general. A syntactic restriction on the distribution of verbs does not allow *shi* to be inserted between a verb and its object, even when the object is strongly focused. The English Focus Marker *be* is also a verb. When finite, a clause will be subject to the subject requirement, so an extra expletive pronoun *it* has to be inserted, although the expletive has nothing to do with focus whatsoever.

6.5 Summary

Starting with some minimal assumptions about "Focus," in this chapter we argue that this initially semantic/pragmatic conception of "Focus" can be taken as a purely formal syntactic feature, and that this formal feature is assigned and/or checked to certain sentential constituents at the DS level of syntactic representation. "Focus" should be divided into two relative categories: Strong Focus [+Fs] and Weak Focus [+Fw]. While the feature [+Fw] generally triggers some phonological process, such as the assignment of primary stress, the feature [+Fs] normally triggers various syntactic processes in natural languages. A language typology has been established about the syntactic processing of [+Fs] by which there are two devices of [+Fs] processing: the insertion of the Focus Marker *be* before focused constituents, and the fronting of focused constituents. English represents the third type of language, which makes use of both devices. Other superficially complex, cross-linguistic differences have been shown to follow from the choice between these two limited options in interaction with independently needed principles.

On the assumption that *Wh*-phrases are all marked [+Fs] in the lexicon and they automatically carry this mark into the phrase marker, we also have argued that there is virtually no such thing as "*Wh*-Movement" in the formal syntax of English. What is called "*Wh*-Movement" is shown to be, in fact, an instantiation of a more generally applicable rule "Focus-Fronting" in English *Wh*-questions. The so-called "Question Formation" is thus decomposed into two independent processes: "Subject-Auxiliary Inversion" and "Focus Fronting." Only the former is a syntactic process triggered by the abstract question morpheme [+Wh], while the latter has nothing to do with either question or question formation whatsoever.

Chapter 7

Focus-Marking in Chinese and Malay[*]

ABSTRACT: *Cross-linguistically, there are two devices for grammar to process the focus feature [+Focus]: the movement of focused constituents and the insertion of a Focus Marker, such as the English "be" before focused constituents. In this mode of formulation, a comparative study of Focus and Focus-Marking in Chinese and Malay has been conducted. These two languages have certain similarities and differences: They are similar in opting for the use of a Focus Marker instead of focused constituent movement; they are different in the nature of the Focus Marker itself. The Focus marker is the copular verb SHI in Chinese, but, as the Malay language simply does not have a copular verb, two complementary particles KAH/LAH are chosen, and all other contrasts in Focus-Marking between the two languages are demonstrated to from the result of the difference in the nature of Focus Marker as well as some other independently motivated conditions in a modularized theory of grammar.*

---

[*]A version of this chapter originally appeared with the title "Focus-Marking in Chinese and Malay: A Comparative Perspective" in *Language, Information, and Computation: Proceedings of the 17th Pacific Asia Conference on Language, Information and Computation* (2003). Revisions made are technical and minimal, the essential contents remain unchanged. It is included in this monograph as a chapter with kind permission from the Chinese and Oriental Languages Information Processing Society, Singapore.

7.1 Introduction

As noted in Chapter 6 of this book, "Focus"-related issues have been studied from different perspectives. We assume that the essentially semantic conception of "Focus" can be characterized as a purely formal syntactic feature [+F], which gets assigned to constituents at a certain level of syntactic representation, triggering such syntactic operations such as "Movement" and "Adjoining" under the general syntactic principles and constraints.

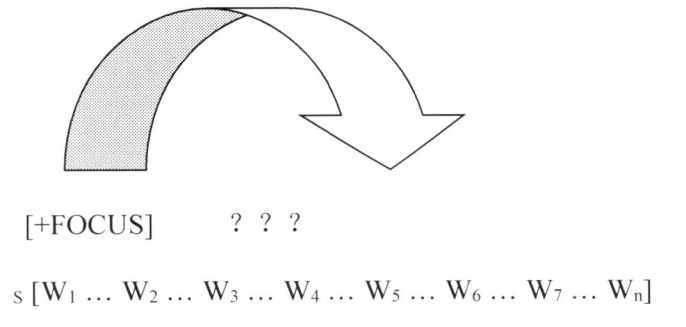

[+FOCUS]   ? ? ?

$_s [W_1 \ldots W_2 \ldots W_3 \ldots W_4 \ldots W_5 \ldots W_6 \ldots W_7 \ldots W_n]$

Although every sentence, by definition, has at least one focused constituent, degree of focalization (i.e. the degree of emphasis) on constituents may vary from one sentence to another. It is reasonable to assume that there are two types of Focus that are formal-linguistically relevant: "Strong Focus" ("[+Fs]") and "Weak Focus" ("[+Fw]"). As argued in the previous chapter, this information must be available at D-Structure to trigger relevant syntactic operations in the course of the derivation from D-Structure to S-Structure.

Cross-linguistically, there are two types of devices for grammar to process the focus feature [+F], especially the strong focus feature [+Fs]: the movement of focused constituents and the insertion of a Focus Marker, such as the English "be" before focused constituents. In this mode of formulation, a comparative study of Chinese and Malay can be conducted since they are both good examples of Focus-Marking languages. They differ minimally in which lexical elements have been taken from the lexicon to serve the purpose of marking the focused constituents.

7.2 Copular Verb *Shi* as a Focus Marker in Chinese

As discussed in chapter 6 of this book, the feature [+F], resulting from Focus-Assignment, may trigger phonological or/and syntactic operations. The phonological operations of [+F], such as primary stress and higher pitch have been noted in the literature (e.g. Jackendoff (1972), and Culicover and Rochemont (1983), among others). As for syntactic operations, the most conceivable one is simply to insert an overt Focus Marker in the sentence, whatever the marker may be in a particular language. Chinese, along with all other Chinese dialects, is a perfect example of a Focus-Marking language. Please see the examples below.

(1) <u>Shi</u> wo mingtian cheng huoche qu Guangzhou.
     SHI I   tomorrow ride train   go Guangzhou
     "I will go to Guangzhou by train tomorrow/
     It is I who will go to Guangzhou by train tomorrow."

(2) Wo <u>shi</u> mingtian cheng huoche qu Guangzhou.
     I   SHI tomorrow ride train   go Guangzhou
     "I will go to Guangzhou by train TOMORROW/
     It is tomorrow when I will go to Guangzhou by train."

(3) Wo mingtian <u>shi</u> cheng huoche qu Guangzhou.
     I   tomorrow SHI ride train   go Guangzhou
     "I will go to Guangzhou BY TRAIN tomorrow /
     It is by train that I will go to Guangzhou tomorrow."

(4) wo mingtian cheng huoche <u>shi</u> qu Guangzhou.
     I   tomorrow ride train   SHI go Guangzhou
     "I will go to GUANGZHOU by train tomorrow/
     It is to Guangzhou that I will go by train tomorrow."

Shi, a copular verb, which literally means "to be," is used to single out a constituent and emphasize it in Chinese. Generally speaking, *shi* can be inserted before any constituent, except for the object NP of a verb or a preposition, to emphasize the constituent, hence sentences (5) and (6) are ungrammatical. Also, since it is a verb in terms of part of speech, *shi*, when used a Focus Marker, exhibits a full set of features of regular verbs of the language. For example, it may enter the so-called "V-neg-V" questions as in (7) below; it can be negated by a negative adverb such as *bu* "not" as in (8).

(5) *Wo zuotian zai xuexiao pengjian-le <u>shi</u> ta.
    I   yesterday on campus meet-Asp SHI him
    "Intended meaning: I met HIM on the campus/
    It was him whom I met on the campus yesterday."

(6) *Wo bei <u>shi</u>   ta pian-le.
    I   by SHI him cheat-Asp
    "Intended: I have been cheated by HIM /
    It was him by whom I have cheated."

(7) <u>Shi</u> bu <u>shi</u>   ta zuotian   jie-le   ni de shu?
    SHI not SHI he yesterday borrow-Asp your book
    "Was it he who borrowed your book yesterday?"

(8) Ta bu   <u>shi</u> guai ni.
    he not SHI blame you
    "He does not blame YOU / It is not you that he blames."

In a modularized theory of syntax, the above phenomena are expected. The initial purpose of inserting *shi* is, perhaps, just to mark the focused constituent. After being inserted into the sentence, however, *shi* exhibits those properties of regular copular verbs. We can say that the ungrammaticality of sentences like (5) and (6) has nothing to do with the insertion of *shi* as a Focus Marker. Rather, they are ungrammatical because the NP counts on its preceding verb or preposition for Case-marking. In this process, the adjacency condition is applicable, prohibiting any other grammatical element, including the Focus Marker, from occurring between the Case assignor (P and V) and assignee (object NP).

At noted in Chapter 6, the positioning of the Focus Marker *shi* in linear word order is determined jointly by two factors. [1] As a verb in terms of part of speech, *shi* has to observe all relevant syntactic conditions governing verbs in Chinese. For example, it cannot be inserted between a verb and its object even if the object NP has an [+Fs] mark from DS representation. In this case, *shi* is normally placed immediately before the verb. [2] *Shi* has to be placed as close as possible to the focused constituent in a sentence should applicable conditions allow for this. A single sentence, as noted above, may have two or more focused constituents. Now it should be pointed out that only one of the several focused constituents can be marked overtly with *shi*, a noteworthy language fact captured under "The Unique Strong Focus Condition" (USFC). The following sentences serve to demonstrate the effect of USFC.

(9) *Wo <u>shi</u> zuotian <u>shi</u> zai bangongshi li deng ni.
      I   SHI yesterday SHI in office wait-for you
      "Intended meaning: I waited for you IN THE OFFICE YESTERDAY."

(10) *<u>Shi</u> wo <u>shi</u> mei mai na ben shu.
      SHI I SHI not buy that   book
      "Intended meaning: It was I who did not buy THAT BOOK."

7.3 Focus-Marking in Malay

Further language facts from the Malay language also support our general claims and arguments, which were made on the basis of evidence in Chinese. Very much like Chinese, Malay is also a Focus-Marking language in which focused constituents are marked with *lah* in declarative sentences, as in (11)–(16) below, or *kah* in interrogative sentences, as in (17)–(21). As two choices for a Focus Marker, *lah* and *kah* are in perfect complementary distribution, and can be taken as one underlining morpheme with two superficial morphological/phonological forms.

First, please consider *lah* in declarative sentences:

(11) Saya-<u>lah</u> yang akan pergi ke Kuala Lumpur.
      I-FM who will go to Kuala Lumpur
      "It is I who will go to Kuala Lumpur."

(12) Pada esok-<u>lah</u> akan saya pergi ke Kuala Lumpur dengan keretapi.
on tomorrow-FM will I go to Kuala Lumpur with train
"It is tomorrow when I will go to Kuala Lumpur by train."

(13) Dia-<u>lah</u> yang saya berjumpa di kampus kelmarin.
He-FM who I met at campus yesterday
"It was him whom I met on the campus yesterday."

(14) Abu belajar di bilik itu-<u>lah</u> tadi.
Abu study at room that-FM just-now
"It was in that room that Abu was studying just now."

(15) Abu belajar-<u>lah</u> di bilik itu tadi.
Abu study-FM at room that just-now
"It was studying that Abu did in that room just now."

(16) Abu belajar di bilik itu tadi-<u>lah</u>.
Abu study at room that just-now-FM
"It was just now that Abu was studying in that room."

Examples of *kah* in interrogative sentences are given below. Please note that *kah* could be used in both matrix interrogatives, as that in (17)–(20), or in embedded interrogatives, as that in (21).

(17) Dia itu Abu-<u>kah</u>?
He that Abu-FM
"Is he ABU?"

(18) Kucing-<u>kah</u> awak nampak di situ tadi?
cat-FM you see at there just-now
"Was it a cat that you saw over there just now?"

(19) Kamu mahu kopi-<u>kah</u> atau teh-<u>kah</u>?
you want coffee-FM or tea-FM
"Do you want coffee or tea?"

(20) Siapa-<u>kah</u> guru itu?
who-FM teacher that
"Who is that teacher?"

(21) Dia bertanya orang itu guru-<u>kah</u> atau bukan.
he ask   person that teacher-FM or not
"He asked if that person is a teacher."

The following two sentences constitute a perfect minimal pair where one can see the contrast between the two forms of one Focus Marker, one for declarative and another for interrogative.

(22) Gadis itu guru Ali-<u>lah</u>.
girl   that teacher Ali-FM
"That girl is ALI'S TEACHER."

(23) Gadis itu guru Ali-<u>kah</u>?
girl   that teacher Ali-FM
"Is that girl ALI'S TEACHER?"

"The Unique Strong Focus Condition" (USFC) also applies in Malay, just as it does in Chinese. A simplex Malay sentence can only have one constituent assigned a Strong Focus feature [+Fs], and thus can only have one constituent marked overtly with a Focus Marker. The contrast in acceptability between (24), which is grammatical and (25), which is ungrammatical, illustrates this point.

(24) Amin sakit-<u>kah</u> kelmarin?   (Kader (1981))
Amin sick-FM yesterday
"Was Amin SICK yesterday?"

(25) *Amin sakit-<u>kah</u> kelmarin-<u>kah</u>?
Amin sick-FM yesterday-FM
Intended Meaning: "Was Amin SICK YESTERDAY?"

The sentence in (19), however, seems to be a counter example to USFC, at least superficially, because the interrogative Focus Marker *kah* is used twice. We note that the double Focus Marker phenomenon is restricted to multiple choice interrogatives only, so the USFC is still observed, since even in the sentence, only one single constituent, i.e. the object of verb, is strongly focused. What is special about (19) is only that the single focused constituent is realized as a coordinative noun phrase and the interrogative Focus Marker *kah* is used on both members of the coordinative phrase.

7.4 Deriving the Contrasts in Focus-Marking between Chinese and Malay

Although the two languages pattern similarly in the choice of focus device, and are both Focus-Marking languages, there are still some interesting contrasts between Chinese and Malay in Focus Marking, which demand a proper theoretical explanation.

1. The two languages differ in the choice of Focus Marker. As noted above, the Chinese Focus Marker *shi* is a typical copular verb, but the Malay Focus Marker *lah/kah* is a suffix-like particle or clitic. Since it is a cross-linguistic phenomenon that copular verbs often serve as the Focus Marker, the Chinese choice is perhaps a natural and expected one. The reason the same choice is not made in Malay is simple too. Malay, just like Archaic Chinese, has no copular verb, or at least no fully fledged copular verb. For example, the sentences in (26)–(28) are supposed to be copular sentences in languages like English and modern Chinese, yet no copular verb or comparable item is used.

(26) Azmin pelajar.
   Azmin student
   "Azmin is a student."

(27) Siapa-kah guru itu?
   Who-FM teacher that
   "Who is that teacher?"

(28) Kuala Lumpur ibunegara Malaysia.
   Kuala Lumpur Capital   Malaysia
   "Kuala Lumpur is the capital of Malaysia."

2. With regard to linear ordering, the Chinese Focus Marker is placed before the focused constituent, and as close as possible to the focused constituent, whereas the Malay Focus Marker comes right after the constituent. This is because the Chinese language is, by and large, a head-final language, whereas Malay is largely a head-initial language. In Malay, not only the Focus Marker, but any modifying syntactic elements are placed after the head words.

(29) Azmin berjumpa gadis <u>cantik</u>.
    Azmin met   girl beautiful
    "Azmin met a beautiful girl. "

(30) Bangunan <u>baru</u> lebih mahal.
    Building new more expensive
    "New buildings are more expensive."

(31) Abu belajarlah di bilik <u>itu</u> tadi.
    Abu study-FM at room that just-now
    "It was studying that Abu did in that room just now."

3. Perhaps as a result of properties 1 and 2 above, the insertion of the Malay Focus Marker is subject to different conditions than that of Chinese. For instance, the distribution of the Chinese Focus Marker *shi* is very much restricted. It can be placed only before the subject NP or somewhere between the subject and the main verb, but never between a verb or a preposition and its object, and even when the object NP happens to be focused, the Focus Marker has to be placed before the verb or the preposition rather before the focused object NP. In contrast, since the Malay Focus Marker is just a particle or a clitic, it is used much more freely than its Chinese counterpart. It can be inserted right after an object when the NP in the object position is focused.

(32) Dia-<u>lah</u> yang saya berjumpa di kampus kelmarin.
     He-FM who I   met   at campus yesterday
     "It was him whom I met on the campus yesterday."

(33) Kamu mahu kopi-<u>kah</u> atau teh-<u>kah</u>?
　　You want coffee-FM or tea-FM
　　"Do you want coffee or tea?"

(34) Abu minum air itu-<u>kah</u> tadi?
　　Abu drink water that-FM just-now
　　"Did Abu drink THAT WATER just now?"

(35) Anak itu sudah pergi ke sekolah-<u>kah</u>?　　(Kader 1981)
　　child the already go to school-FM
　　"Was it to school where the child already went?"

(36) Awak beli kereta yang besar itu-<u>kah</u> kelmarin?
　　You　buy car　which big that-FM yesterday
　　"Which big car did you buy yesterday?"

As reported in Shi and Xu (2000), *shi* once weakened a step further and developed into an almost pure *lah/kah*-like Focus Marker, having lost its original property as a copular verb in Middle Chinese. Consequently, such *shi* was not subject to the conditions on verbs and could be placed between a verb and its object, as illustrated by sentences (37) and (38) below.

(37) Wo ji yang   wen, ru wei <u>shi</u> shui. (*Xian Yu Jing*)
　　I then look-up ask you are FM who
　　"I then looked up and asked who you are."

(38) Ci wei <u>shi</u> shui. (*Xian Yu Jing*)
　　This is FM who
　　"Who is this (person)?"

4. Lastly, but most interestingly, Focus-Marking as one type of focus device may be used in conjunction with another (i.e. Focus-Fronting) in Malay, but not in Chinese. As is cross-linguistically generalized in Xu and Li (1993) and in Chapter 6 of this book, there are two devices by which grammar can process the Focus Feature [+Focus]: (i) moving the focused constituent to a more prominent position which may vary from one language to another, and (ii) inserting a Focus Marker either before or after the

focused constituent. English is an interesting language in which the focus devices are used jointly. We find that Malay patterns with English in the joint usage of the two focus devices, but the language differs from English in that Focus-Fronting is obligatory in English but optional in Malay, while Focus-Marking is obligatory in both languages. The sentences in (39)–(42) below illustrate the contrast between English and Malay in whether Focus-Fronting is obligatory or optional after a Focus Marker is inserted. Also, the English Focus Marker, like its Chinese counterpart, is the copular verb *to be*, whereas the Malay Focus Marker is a particle or clitic *lah/kah* as discussed above.[1]

English

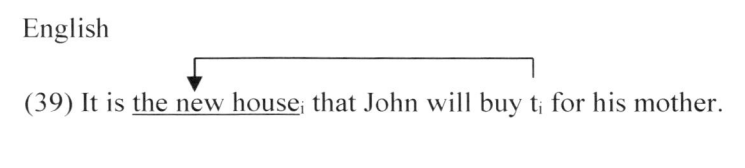

(39) It is <u>the new house</u>$_i$ that John will buy t$_i$ for his mother.

(40) <u>What</u>$_i$ is it that you bought t$_i$ yesterday?

Malay

(41) a. <u>Dia-lah</u>$_i$ yang saya berjumpa t$_i$ di kampus kelmarin.
      he-FM who I   met   at campus yesterday
      "It was him whom I met on the campus yesterday."

   b. Saya berjumpa <u>dia-lah</u> di kampus kelmarin.
      I   met   he-FM at campus yesterday
      "It was him whom I met on the campus yesterday."

(42) a. <u>Kucing-kah</u>$_i$ awak nampak t$_i$ di situ tadi?
      Cat-FM   you see   at there just-now
      "Was it a cat that you saw over there just now?"

   b. Awak nampak <u>kucing-kah</u> di situ tadi?
      you   see   Cat-FM   at there just-now
      "Was it a cat that you saw over there just now?"

7.5 Summary

The focus feature [+FOCUS] may trigger different syntactic operations in different languages. The operations could involve either a movement of the focused constituent (Focus Fronting), or an insertion of a focus marker before or after the focused constituent (Focus-Marking) under the generally applicable syntactic principles and constraints. Chinese and Malay pattern similarly in that they both use a Focus Marker to realize their focused constituent, but contrast minimally in (i) the choice of lexical item used as the Focus Marker: The Focus Marker is the copular verb *shi* in Chinese, whereas two complementary particles *kah/lah* in Malay, which in turn, we argue in this chapter, is due to another simple difference between the two languages: Malay simply does not have a copular verb, and copular verb is most commonly chosen by Chinese and many other languages as a Focus Marker; and (ii) the linear positioning of the Focus Marker: It is placed before focused constituent in Chinese, but comes after focused constituent in Malay. This is due to an independently motivated and generally applicable difference between the two languages: Chinese is a head-final language in which all modifiers, including the Focus Marker, are positioned before their heads; Malay is a head-initial language in which all modifiers are placed after their heads. Furthermore, as suffix-like particles, the Malay Focus Marker *kah/lah* is used much more freely than the Chinese copular verb *shi*. For example, the latter cannot come in between a verb or a preposition and its object but the former can.

Notes

[1] There seems to be another difference between Malay and English in that the pronoun *it* has to be used in addition to the copular verb *be* as a Focus Marker in English, but what is inserted there is simply the Focus Marker *kah/lah* in Malay. We take this to be one of the side effects of the difference in the nature of the Focus Marker rather than as an independent contrast. In English, the initial purpose of the *be* insertion could well be to mark the focused constituent, but it automatically creates a predicate, which, by a condition completely independent of the issue concerning us here, demands an insertion of a "dummy subject" *it* (just as the *it* inserted in *it is raining* and in *it is said that he won't make it*).

References

Aissen, Judith L. (1992) 'Topic and Focus in Mayan,' *Language*, 68.1.

Akmajian, Adrian (1970) 'On Deriving Cleft-Sentences from Pseudo-Cleft Sentences,' *Linguistic Inquiry*, 1.2.

Aoun, Joseph, Norbert Hornstein and Dominique Sportiche (1981) 'Some Aspects of Wide Scope Quantification,' *Journal of Linguistic Research*, 1.3.

Aoun, Joseph (1985) *A Grammar of Anaphora*, Cambridge: The MIT Press.

Aoun, Joseph, Norbert Hornstein, David Lightfoot and Amy Weinberg (1987) 'Two Types of Locality,' *Linguistic Inquiry*, 18.4.

Bach, Emmon (1971) 'Questions,' *Linguistic Inquiry*, 2.2.

Belletti, Adriana (1988) 'The Case of Unaccusatives,' *Linguistic Inquiry*, 19.1.

Bickerton, Derek (1987) 'He Himself: Anaphor, Pronoun, Or...?' *Linguistic Inquiry*, 18.2.

Burzio, Luigi (1986) *Italian Syntax: A Government-Binding Approach*, Dordrecht, Boston, Lancaster and Tokyo: D. Reidel Publishing Company.

Burzio, Luigi (1991) 'Morphological Basis of Anaphora,' *Journal of Linguistics*, 27.1.

Campos, Hector (1986) 'Indefinite Object Drop,' *Linguistic Inquiry*, 17.2.

Chao, Yuan Ren (1968) *A Grammar of Spoken Chinese*, Berkeley and Los Angeles: University of California Press.

Chen, Chung-yu (1993) *Aspects of Mandarin Chinese*, Singapore: Chinese Language and Research Centre, National University of Singapore.

Choi, Young-Seok (1988) *A Study of Ascension Constructions in Korean*, Doctoral Dissertation, University of Hawaii.

Chomsky, Noam (1980) 'On Binding,' *Linguistic Inquiry*, 11.1.

Chomsky, Noam (1981) *Lectures on Government and Binding*, Dordrecht: Foris Publications.

Chomsky, Noam (1986) *Knowledge of Language: Its Nature, Origin, and Use*, New York: Praeger.

Chomsky, Noam and Howard Lasnik (1993) 'The Theory of Principles and Parameters,' in J. Jacbos, A. von Stechow, W. Sternefeld, and T. Vennemann (eds.) *Syntax: An International Handbook of Contemporary Research*, Berlin and New York: Walter de Gruyter.

Chomsky, Noam (1995) *The Minimalist Program*, Cambridge University Press.

Chomsky, Noam (2002) *The Nature and Language*, Cambridge: The MIT Press.

Cole, Peter (1987) 'Null Objects in Universal Grammar,' *Linguistic Inquiry*, 17.4.

Cole, Peter, Gabriella Hermon and Li-May Sung (1990) 'Principles and Parameters of Long-Distance Reflexives,' *Linguistic Inquiry*, 21.1.

Cole, Peter and Li-May Sung (1990) *Feature Percolation in GB Theory*, Ms., University of Delaware.

Culicover, Peter W. and Michael S. Rochemont (1983) 'Stress and focus in English,' *Language*, 59.1.

Culicover, Peter W. (1991) 'Topicalization, Inversion, and Complementizers in English,' Ms., Columbus: The Ohio State University.

De Rijk, Rudolf P. G. (1978) 'Topic Fronting, Focus Positioning and the Nature of Verb Phrase in Basque,' in F. Jansen (ed.) *Studies on Fronting*, Lisse: Peter de Ridder Press.

Epstein, Samuel David (1984) 'A Note on Functional Determination and Strong Crossover,' *The Linguistic Review*, 3.3.

Fang, Huanhai (1998) 'Shenme' Yuyuan de Fangyan Buzheng (Some Justification from Chinese Dialects about the Etymology of 'Shenme'), *Zhongguo Yuwen*, No.4.

Fang, Mei (1995) Hanyu Duibi Jiaodian de Jufa Biaoxian Shouduan (Syntactic Behaviors of Contrastive Focus in Chinese), *Zhongguo Yuwen*, No. 4.

Farrel, Patrick (1990) 'Null Objects in Brazilian Portuguese,' *Natural Language and Linguistic Theory*, 8.3.

Feng, Shengli (1997) *Hanyu de Yunlu, Cifa yu Jufa* (Prosody, Morphology and Syntax in Chinese), Beijing: Peking University Press.

Fiengo, Robert, James Cheng-Teh Huang, Howard Lasnik and Tanya Reinhart (1988) 'The Syntax of Wh-in-situ,' in *Proceedings of the 7th West Coast Conference on formal Linguistics*, Stanford: CSLI Publications.

Fukui, Naoki and Margaret Speas (1986) 'Specifiers and Projection,' *MIT Working Papers in Linguistics*, 8.

Gundel, Jeanette K. (1999) 'On Different Kinds of Focus,' in Peter Bosch and Rob van der Sandt (eds.) *Focus: Linguistic, Cognitive, and Computational Perspectives*, Cambridge and New York: Cambridge University Press.

Higginbotham, James and Robert May (1981) 'Questions, Quantifiers and Crossing,' *The Linguistic Review*, 1.1.

Horvath, Julia (1986) *FOCUS in the Theory of Grammar and the Syntax of Hungarian*, Dordrecht: Foris Publications.

Huang, Cheng-Teh James (1982a) 'Move Wh in a Language without Wh-Movement,' *The Linguistic Review*, 1.4.

Huang, Cheng-Teh James (1982b) *Logical Relations in Chinese and the Theory of Grammar*, Doctoral Dissertation, MIT, Cambridge, Massachusetts.

Huang, Cheng-Teh James (1984a) 'On the Distribution and Reference of Empty Pronouns,' *Linguistic Inquiry*, 15.4.

Huang, Cheng-Teh James (1984b) 'On the Typology of Zero Anaphora,' *Language Research*, 20.2.

Huang, Cheng-Teh James (1987) 'Remarks on Empty Categories in Chinese,' *Linguistic Inquiry*, 18.2.

Huang, Cheng-Teh James and Chih-Chen Jane Tang (1988) 'On the Local Nature of Long-Distance Reflexive in Chinese,' in *Proceedings of the 18th annual meeting of the North East Linguistics Society*, University of Massachusetts-Amherst.

Huang, Cheng-Teh James (1989) Shuo Shi he You (On Shi and You), in *A Collection of Papers in Honour of Professor Fang-Kui Li*, Taipei.

Huang, Dinghua (1963) Minnan Fangyan li de Yiwen Daici (Question Words in the Southern Min Dialect), Zhongguo Yuwen, No. 4.

Hu, Jianhua and Haihua Pan (2000) 'Deriving the Subject-object Asymmetry in Topicalization,' paper presented at International Symposium on Topic and Focus in Chinese, The Hong Kong Polytechnic University.

Hyams, Nina (1986) *Language Acquisition and the Theory of Parameters*, Dordrecht, Boston, Lancaster, and Tokyo: D. Reidel Publishing Company.

Hyams, Nina (1989) 'The Null Subject Parameter in Language Acquisition,' in O. Jaeggli and K. Safir (1989).

Jackendoff, Ray S. (1972) Semantic Interpretation in Generative Grammar, Cambridge: The MIT Press.

Jaeggli, Osvaldo A. (1982) *Topics in Romance Syntax*, Dordrecht: Foris Publications.

Jaeggli, Osvaldo A. (1986) 'Passive,' Linguistic Inquiry, 17.4.

Jaeggli, Osvaldo A. and Kenneth J. Safir (1989) (eds.) *The Null Subject Parameter*, Dordrecht: Kluwer Academic Publishers.

Kader, Mashudi B. H. (1981) *The Syntax of Malay Interrogatives*, Kuala Lumpur: Dewan Bahasa dan Pustaka.

Kang, Myung-Yoon (1987) 'Possessor Raising in Korean,' in S. Kuno, I. W. Lee and Y. S. Kang (eds.) *Harvard Studies in Korean Linguistics II*, Seoul: Hanshin.

Kayne, Richard S. (1981) 'On Certain Differences between French and English,' *Linguistic Inquiry*, 12.3.

Kazman, Rick (1988) 'Null Arguments and the Acquisition of Case and Infl,' Paper presented at the Boston University Conference on Language Acquisition, Boston University.

Kitagawa, Yoshihisa (1986) *Subjects in Japanese and English*, Doctoral Dissertation, University of Massachusetts-Amherst.

Kuno, Susumu (1973) *The Structure of the Japanese Language*, Cambridge: The MIT Press.

LaPolla, Randy J. (1993) 'Pragmatic Relations and Word Order in Chinese,' in Pamela Downing and Michael Noonam (eds.) *Word Order in Discourse*, Amsterdam and Philadelphia: John Benjamins Publishing Company.

Larson, Richard K. (1988) 'On the Double Object Construction,' *Linguistic Inquiry*, 19.3.

Lasnik, Howard and Mamoru Saito (1984) 'On the Nature of Proper Government,' *Linguistic Inquiry*, 15.2.

Lebeaux, David (1983) 'A Distributional Difference between Reflexives and Reciprocals,' *Linguistic Inquiry*, 14.2.

Lebeaux, David (1988) *Language Acquisition and the Form of the Grammar*, Doctoral Dissertation, University of Massachusetts-Amherst.

Lebeaux, David (1991) 'Relative Clauses, Licensing, and the Nature of the Derivation,' in S. Rothstein and M. Speas (eds.) *Syntax and Semantics 25: Phrase Structure, Heads and Licensing*, New York: Academic Press.

Li, Charles N. and Sandra A. Thompson (1976) 'Subject and Topic: A New Typology,' in C. Li (ed.) *Subject and Topic*, New York: Academic Press.

Li, Charles N. and Sandra A. Thompson (1981) *Mandarin Chinese: A Functional Reference Grammar*, Berkeley and Los Angeles: University of California Press.

Lightfoot, David (1989) 'The Child's Trigger Experience: Degree-0 Learnability,' *Behavioral and Brain Sciences*, 12.2.

Lightfoot, David (1991) *How to Set Parameters: Arguments from Language Change*, Cambridge: The MIT Press.

Lightfoot, David (1995) 'Why UG Needs a Learning Theory: Triggering Verb Movement,' in A. Battye and I. Roberts (eds.) *Clause Structure and Language Change*, New York: Oxford University Press.

Lightfoot, David (1999) *The Development of Language: Acquisition, Change, and Evolution*, Oxford: Blackwell Publishers.

Li, Mei-Du (1985) *Reduction and Anaphoric Relations in Chinese*, Doctoral Dissertation, University of California, San Diego.

Li, Yen-Hui Audrey (1985) *Abstract Cases in Chinese*, Doctoral Dissertation, University of Southern California, Los Angeles.

Lu, Shuxiang (1985) *Jindai Hanyu Zhidaici* (Referential Pronouns in Early Mandarin), Shanghai: Xuelin Press.

Nishigauchi, T. (1985) *Japanese LF: In defense of Subjacency*, Kobe mimeo.

Ni, Weijia (1987) 'Empty Topics in Chinese,' in *UConn Working Papers in Linguistics* 1, University of Connecticut, Storrs.

O'Grady, William (1991) *Categories and Case: The Sentence Structure of Korean*, Amsterdam: John Benjamins.

Ouhalla, Jamal (1991) *Functional Categories and Parametric Variation*, London: Routledge.

Perlmutter, David M. (1978) 'Impersonal Passives and the Unaccusative Hypothesis,' in *Proceedings of the 4th Annual Meeting of the Berkeley Linguistic Society*, 38.

Radford, Andrew (1981) *Transformational Syntax*, Cambridge: Cambridge University Press.

Raposo, Eduardo (1986) 'On the Null Objects in European Portuguese,' in *Studies in Romance Linguistics*, Dordrecht: Foris Publications.

Rizzi, Luigi (1982) *Issues in Italian Syntax*, Dordrecht: Foris Publications.

Rizzi, Luigi (1990) 'Speculations on Verb Second,' in Mascaro and M. Nespor (eds.) *Grammar in Progress: GLOW Essays for Henk van Riemsdijk*, Dordrecht: Foris Publications.

Roberts, Ian G. (1985) 'Agreement Parameters and the Development of English Modal Auxiliaries,' *Natural Language and Linguistic Theory*, 3.1.

Rochemont, Michael S. and Peter W. Culicover (1990) *English Focus Constructions and the Theory of Grammar*, Cambridge: Cambridge University Press.

Rouveret, Alain and Jean-Roger Vergnaud (1980) 'Specifying Reference to the Subject: French Causatives and Conditions on Representations,' *Linguistic Inquiry*, 11.1.

Shi, Dingxu (2000) 'The Nature of Background Topic,' paper presented at International Symposium on Topic and Focus in Chinese, The Hong Kong Polytechnic University.

Tang, Sze-Wing and Thomas Hun-tak Lee (2000) 'Focus as an Anchoring Condition,' paper presented at International Symposium on Topic and Focus in Chinese, The Hong Kong Polytechnic University.

Taraldsen, Tarald (1978) 'On the NIC, Vacuous Application, and the *That*-trace Filter,' Ms., MIT. (Reproduced in 1980 by the Indiana University Linguistics Club as 'On the Nominative Island Condition, Vacuous Application, and the *That*-Trace Filter')

Tateishi, Koichi (1994) *The Syntax of 'Subjects'*, Stanford: CSLI Publications.

Teng, Shou-Hsin (1979) 'Remarks on Cleft Sentences in Chinese,' *Journal of Chinese Linguistics*, 7.1.

Thompson, Sandra A. (1973) 'Transitivity and the Ba Construction in Mandarin Chinese,' *Journal of Chinese Linguistics*, 7.1.

Tsai, Wei-Tien Dylan (2000) 'Object Fronting and Focus Placement in Chinese,' paper presented at International Symposium on Topic and Focus in Chinese, The Hong Kong Polytechnic University.

Wang, Li (1958) *Hanyu Shigao* (A History of the Chinese Language), Beijing: Science Press.

Weinberg, Amy (1991) 'Markedness Versus Maturation: The Case of Subject-Auxiliary Inversion,' *Language Acquisition*, 1.2.

Xing, Fuyi (1981) Xiandai Hanyu li de Yi Zhong Shuang Zhuyu Jushi (A Sentence Pattern with Double Subjects in Modern Chinese), *Yuyan Yanjiu*, No. 1.

Xing, Fuyi (1996) *Hanyu Yufaxue* (A Grammar of the Chinese Language), Changchun: Northeast Normal University Press.

Xu, Jie (1993a) 'Possessor Raising in Chinese Passive and Ergative Constructions,' *University of Maryland Working Papers in Linguistics*, 1.

Xu, Jie (1993b) *An Infl Parameter and Its Consequences*, Doctoral Dissertation, University of Maryland at College Park.

Xu, Jie (2001) *Grammatical Principles and Grammatical Phenomena*, Beijing: Peking University Press.

Xu, Jie (2003) *Sentence Head and Sentence Structure: A Study with Special Reference to Chinese*, Singapore: Longman.

Xu, Jie (2004) Yuyi shang de Tongzhi Guanxi yu Jufa shang de Shuang Binyu Jushi (The Semantic Relationship of Co-reference and the Syntactic Construction of Double Objects), *Zhongguo Yuwen*, No. 4.

Xu, Jie and Ying-che Li (1993) Jiaodian he Liangge Fei Xiangxing Yufa Fanchou (Focus and the Two Non-Linear Grammatical Categories: '+Neg' and '+Wh'), *Zhongguo Yuwen*, No. 2.

Xu, Liejiong and D. Terence Langendoen (1985) 'Topic Structures in Chinese,' *Language*, 61.1.

Xu, Liejiong (1986) 'Free Empty Category,' *Linguistic Inquiry*, 17.1.

Xu, Liejiong (2000) 'Association between Operator and Focus,' paper presented at International Symposium on Topic and Focus in Chinese, The Hong Kong Polytechnic University.

Yang, Suying (2000) 'The Presence or Absence of Identificational Focus in the Shi ... (de) Construction,' paper presented at International Symposium on Topic and Focus in Chinese, The Hong Kong Polytechnic University.

Zagona, Karen (1982) *Government and Proper Government of Verbal Projections*, Doctoral Dissertation, University of Washington, Seattle.

Index

adjacency condition, 73, 109

adverbial, 55, 57–58, 66

anaphor, 55

    Local anaphor, 57

    subject anaphor, 99

BA-Construction, 17–20, 51

Binding Condition, 55, 121, 123, 136

    Generalized Binding, 112

Case, 35–37, 39, 44, 51

    Assignment of Case by verbal trace, 12, 14–15, 29–30, 39, 44, 51

    Case Filter, 105–106, 108

    double Accusative Case, 7–12, 51–52

    Generalized Case Filter (GCF), 105–106, 108, 115

    Partitive Case, 3–4, 30, 34, 39

Cleft sentence, 65, 70, 158, 161

Complex Noun Phrase Constraint (CNPC), 65, 69, 135

double nominative construction, 26, 51

double object construction, 8–9, 33

double subject construction, 26, 47

Empty Category Principle (ECP), 66, 70, 111, 118

    functional determination theory of empty category, 127–128, 135

ergative construction, 2–3, 6, 51

expletive, 93–94, 96, 98, 161

feature percolation, 132

focus, 142

    focus assignment, 142–143, 147, 162, 171

    focus clitic, 177–178, 181

focus construction, 70, 75, 85
focus feature, 142, 181
Focus-Fronting, 151, 156, 159, 162, 165, 179, 181
focus marker, 64, 67, 71–75, 85, 143–148, 160, 167, 171–173, 177
Focus-Marking, 143, 147, 159, 172, 181
Language Typology of Focus, 168
strong focus, 143–146, 149–150, 156–157, 169, 171, 176
Unique Strong Focus Condition (USFC), 148, 150, 174, 176
weak focus, 143–146, 169, 171
Generalized Control Rule (GCR), 103, 117, 123, 132, 134
Generalized Control Rule Parameter (GCRP), 124
INFL, 23–24, 26, 51, 62, 67, 90
INFL Government Parameter (IGP), 123
INFL Parameter, 90, 97, 99, 105, 115
Lexical INFL, 110–112, 115
Lexical INFL Hypothesis, 67
Locality Condition, 44, 62, 64, 66, 70, 74, 78, 85–86, 127, 160
Logical Form (LF), 64, 86
LF-movement, 60, 64–66, 74, 77–78, 82, 112–113
long-distance binding, 57
Morphological Uniformity (MU), 104
multiple nominative construction, 90, 99
nominative Case, 91–93, 99, 105
null object, 117–118, 123–124, 128, 131, 133
null subject, 92, 94–100, 115
null subject parameter, 102, 104
null topic, 122, 124
object preposing, 151–152
passive construction, 2–3, 6, 28–29, 43, 49, 51
Pied-Piping, 64, 86, 88
Possessor Raising, 2, 4, 44, 49
landing site of Possessor Raising, 2, 6, 26
preposition stranding, 108
presupposition, 142
Principle of Licensing Well-Formedness, 71, 94, 147
pro, 117, 125, 128, 131–132

question, 65, 72
    question formation, 163, 169
reciprocal, 60–63
reflexive, 55, 57, 60
    long-distance reflexive, 112
resumptive pronoun, 42, 160
Subjacency Condition, 2, 26, 45, 47, 51, 66, 69–70, 85, 117–127, 130
Subject-Auxiliary Inversion (SAI), 164–166, 169
subject-object asymmetry, 117–121, 125, 128, 135
Subject Raising, 20, 49–50
Subject-/Topic-Prominent Language Typology, 24, 91
That-trace effect, 110–111
Topic construction, 85, 91, 99, 127
Unaccusative Hypothesis, 4
V-Raising, 9, 29–30
Wh-movement, 162

Printed in the United States
By Bookmasters